God Keeps His PROMISES

Trusting in the One Who is Faithful
When Vows are Broken

CHRISTY LONG

God Keeps His Promises by Christy Long
Copyright © 2008 by Christy Long
All Rights Reserved.
ISBN: 1-59755-177-5

Published by: ADVANTAGE BOOKS™
                www.advbookstore.com

This book and parts thereof may not be reproduced in any form, stored in a retrieval system or transmitted in any form by any means (electronic, mechanical, photocopy, recording or otherwise) without prior written permission of the author, except as provided by United States of America copyright law.

NOTE: Many of the names of individuals in this book have been changed to fictitious names in order to protect their identities. This is a true story and the people and quotes mentioned in the book are real; only the names have been changed.

Unless otherwise indicated, Scripture quotations are taken from the *Holy Bible, New International Version*, NIV. Copyright 1973, 1978, 1984 by International Bible Society. Used by permission of Zondervan Publishing House. All rights reserved.

Scripture quotations marked NLT are taken from the Holy Bible, New Living Translation, copyright 1996. Used by permission of Tyndale House Publishers, Inc., Wheaton, IL 60189 USA. All rights reserved.

Library of Congress Control Number: 2008940164

Cover design by Pat Theriault

First Printing: November 2008
08 09 10 11 12 13 14 10 9 8 7 6 5 4 3 2
Printed in the United States of America

Dedications

To Madison, Jackson, and Bryson – You are my precious gifts from God!

To Mark – Thank you for being the godly man that you are and for loving *all* of us!

To Mama and Daddy – I couldn't have gotten through the tough times without your love and support!

To Grandma Dot and Pap-Paw – Although you are now both in heaven with our Lord, I pray that you know how much I love and appreciate all you did for me while here on this earth. See you in a little while!

Christy Long

Table of Contents

Foreword 7

Acknowledgments 9

Introduction 11

Chapter One 15
Who Am I?

Chapter Two 27
Unanswered Prayers

Chapter Three 41
My God, My Great Provider

Chapter Four 53
Security Check

Chapter Five 63
Hope and a Future

Chapter Six 87
Been There, Done That

Chapter Seven 105
Your Will, Not Mine

Chapter Eight 115
Blessed Beyond Measure

Chapter Nine 125
Desires of My Heart

Chapter Ten 137
Healer of My Heart

Endnotes 151

Foreword

God does not abandon His children on the day they divorce. Christians struggle with divorce and rightly so. The Scriptures are clear that divorce is not God's design. God's plan is one man, married to one woman, for a lifetime. Marriage is to be a loving relationship where each looks out for the well-being of the other. When this plan is followed, marriage reaches its intended potential.

However, God also has given us freedom. Yes, even freedom to walk away from His plans for us. When a husband or a wife violates the marriage covenant by sexual immorality and refuses to repent and seek restoration, divorce is the result. The scriptures say that it is the "hardness of our hearts" that leads to divorce. We refuse to repent and seek forgiveness. We continue in our sinful ways and in so doing, we create divorce.

Often, one spouse is willing to forgive and the other is not open to reconciliation. The one who desires reconciliation cannot keep their spouse from pursuing divorce. For the Christian this is a time of great pain, similar to the pain which God experiences when we refuse to be reconciled to Him.

Many readers will identify with the emotions that Christy experienced in her own journey through divorce. Her story demonstrates that God's plan for us does not end when our spouse walks away. God is our redeemer. He is acquainted with pain, and He will never forsake us. We cannot control the behavior of our spouse, but we can choose to put our hand in God's hand and trust Him with our future. Thanks Christy for sharing your story.

Gary D. Chapman
Author of *The Five Love Languages* and *Love As a Way of Life*

Christy Long

Acknowledgments

I would like to express my deep appreciation to Dr. Gary Chapman and his wife Karolyn, for not only taking time out of their very busy schedule to read my manuscript, but also for the extra time Dr. Chapman took to personally meet with me and provide feedback and helpful information about publishing options. He is a true servant of God and we are blessed to have him on staff at our church.

A special thank you goes to Tricia Kube for her kindness and encouraging words. Her personal interest in simply wanting to read my manuscript meant a great deal to me.

I would like to especially thank my friends and family members who initially read and/or proofread my manuscript, offered valuable input that made the content better, and ultimately played an important role in getting it ready for print – Julie Barney, Alysia Grimes, Martha Morrison; my parents, Jerry and Avalene Pegram; and my husband, Mark.

A huge thank you goes to my parents, Jerry and Avalene Pegram, who so graciously and willingly provided the funds to put this book into print. Thank you for believing in the message God put on my heart and for making it possible to reach others.

Our small prayer group and friends, Kent and Julie Barney, and Andy and Marsha Kunkel must also be mentioned. A few months ago, this project was in the infant stages of writing. I had a book on my heart; and as I shared my dream with them one November evening in our living room, they prayed for me and continued to pray throughout the process – that I would find time to write, that it would be God's story and His will would be done, and that it would bring Him glory. Thank you my brothers and sisters in Christ, for your prayers, encouragement, and accountability!

Introduction

"Praise be to the God and Father of our Lord Jesus Christ, the Father of compassion and the God of all comfort who comforts us in all our troubles, so that we can comfort those in any trouble with the comfort we ourselves have received from God." 2 Corinthians 1:3-4

As I begin writing my story, I want to explain that it has been on my heart for a long time to tell of what God has done for me. When I became a single mom after a bitter divorce several years ago, I was brought to my knees; and through the painful circumstances I went through, learned to totally depend on my Lord and Savior, Jesus Christ. Since that time, I have sadly learned of so many others who have suffered the pain of separation or another major loss, even the death of a loved one. While I did suffer for a time, God has most certainly revealed that He had a wonderful plan for my life.

"And the God of all grace, who called you to his eternal glory in Christ, after you have suffered *a little while*, will himself restore you and make you strong, firm and steadfast."
1 Peter 5:10 (Italics mine)

At the time of my suffering, I could never have imagined the miraculous ways God would work in my life. More importantly, this period of testing was used to make me stronger in my faith. I had never learned to totally rely on God to meet all of my needs until that time. My purpose is to let others know of the hope they can have in Jesus Christ. No matter what trial we are going through, if we put our trust in Him, and are obedient to His word, He will never forsake us.

I think it is important to mention that it has been seven years since my separation. I was seven months pregnant with our second child when my husband left, and it was by far the worst experience of my life up until that point. While I have made several attempts to write my story over the course of the last three to four years, I do not believe it was yet God's timing. Seven is His perfect number as can be found throughout Scripture, and I believe it took seven years for my heart to be completely healed in order for me to convey the message the way that He wants me to. Some of my past attempts were more about what was done *to me* rather than what God has done *for me*.

I will confess that originally I felt it was my mission to tell everyone what had been done to me. While telling it to a counselor or a Christian friend or family member would have been a healthy thing to do, it was certainly not a godly example to "air my dirty laundry" and slander my ex-husband. **Colossians 5:8** tells us, **"But now you must rid yourselves of all such things as these: anger, rage, malice, slander, and filthy language from your lips."** When I was growing up, I remember hearing my grandma say, *"If you can't say something nice about somebody, don't say anything at all!"* We all heard it when we were children, but what a practical, common sense reminder to guard our tongues! It took a long time for me to get over what happened. I also believe that I needed to "justify" to others why I was divorced, because I never wanted to be a divorced person. I always believed (and still do) that a man and woman are supposed to stay married for life. In fact, God himself says in **Malachi 2:16, *"I hate divorce."*** However, if one person wants out of the marriage, the other spouse cannot change his or her heart. Sometimes, in order for a marriage to survive, there must be true brokenness and a willingness to change before the forgiveness, healing, and reconciliation can begin. If there is not true sorrow over the wrong that has been committed, how can there ever again be trust? No matter what the circumstances, I should not have talked negatively about my ex-husband or anyone else. I certainly did not always handle the situation in a Christ-like way, but God has done a tremendous work of healing in my heart and I have been spiritually refined through the process and have matured in my faith as a result.

Today, I truly do not have feelings of bitterness anymore and would consider the relationship with my ex-husband and his wife and his family to be good. Only by the grace of God could this be possible! It has taken about seven years to be able to write my story without including any unnecessary information that would only have caused more hurt or bad feelings.

It has also taken about seven years for God to keep working in my life – or I should say this chapter in my life. Thank goodness He's still not finished with *me*! Even though I had tried to write several times before, not only was my heart not yet ready, but God had not yet finished what He was doing as part of my testimony. He has blessed us so much in the last couple of years and I now know it is His intent for me to include those blessings in this book. He has truly given me the **"desires of my heart"** as the Bible says in Psalm 37:4. Just because *God hates divorce,* it is extremely important that we divorced Christians do not misunderstand that to mean that *Jesus no longer loves us.* **"Who shall separate us from the** love of Christ? Shall trouble or hardship or persecution or famine or nakedness or danger or sword?"** Romans 8:35** *Not even divorce*, Satan's destruction of God's covenant marriage, can separate us from the love of Jesus. If He can forgive us, then we must forgive each other as well as ourselves. Please hear me when I say, **"There is now no condemnation for those who are in Christ Jesus." Romans 8:1**

Finally, Satan has definitely done his best to make me feel totally unworthy to write my story. It seems I constantly battle the voices in my head that say, *"Nobody wants to hear about your story,"* or *"What makes you think you are qualified to write?", "You're only wasting your time; no one will ever publish this."* The devil would love for me to procrastinate and keep my personal testimony hidden in my heart. He delights in my fear and would take pleasure in my remaining silent. At this very moment, I do not know if this will ever be published, but I do know that I want to write down my life testimony, if only for my children to read. If this never makes it to print, it will serve to teach my children how great our God is and how much He has blessed our family. I have also included several life applications that I wish I had personally followed during my separation/divorce process. I learned some hard lessons as I struggled through this major life trial and have given some prayerful consideration to the insight that I may be able to pass along to another person undergoing a similar trial. It is my prayer that should anyone choose to read this, he or she will be touched by my story and I could only hope that I could one day say, just as the apostle Paul said, **"…that what has happened to me has really served to advance the gospel." Philippians 1:12** If only one person would learn to trust Jesus Christ as Lord and Savior through my story, then it would all be worth it.

God Keeps His Promises

Chapter One

Who Am I?

"Not that we are competent in ourselves to claim anything for ourselves, but our competence comes from God." 2 Corinthians 3:5

As an only child and only grandchild growing up in a mid-sized North Carolina town, life was mostly good. I had never known what it was like to go without anything. I always had fashionable, designer clothes, enjoyed eating out at nice restaurants with my parents, and was even allowed to take a friend with me on vacation. Some might even say I was *spoiled*! To be honest, I really never appreciated how good I had it. I was an eighties child. In my household, the Reagan years were prosperous years. My parents, Jerry and Avalene Pegram, were among the last generation of blue collar workers to do well for themselves in the corporate world. My dad worked as a lab technician for a brewery and my mom was a secretary for a local tobacco company. She eventually worked her way up to Senior Executive Assistant to the CEO of Tobacco International. I used to jokingly say that *beer and cigarettes* put me through college.

While cigarettes have certainly come under fire the last few years, this particular company used to be *the best* place to work in town. The tobacco company was good to my family for several generations as my grandfather and great-grandfather retired from there.

The town in which I live is also home to a Moravian settlement where you can take a tour back in time. My family belonged to one of the Moravian churches in town – the home church of my grandmother and great-grandmother. I was christened in that church as a baby, and later confirmed when I was around 12 years old. Confirmation basically comes after a series of catechism classes where you learn about the beliefs and history of the church, and then acknowledge before the congregation your belief in Jesus Christ as the Son of God and your Savior. I had attended Sunday school and Bible school as a child and from the time I could remember I always believed in Jesus.

Later, during my pre-teen years, my family changed our church membership to another Moravian church closer to our home. I was friends with kids from school who attended that church and I became involved in the youth group there. I was a good kid; I really never got into trouble. My parents taught me right from wrong and I was obedient for the most part, but I really wasn't growing spiritually. I was too wrapped up in the various teenage soap operas going on in my life.

In 1988, I graduated from high school and left for college at Appalachian State University in the mountains of Boone, North Carolina. I have to say, I had pretty much been sheltered my entire life, so freedom was a bit scary. As it turned out, I was extremely homesick my first semester. I had a dear roommate who never seemed to leave the room. I believe she was a little afraid of being alone and therefore she seemed to stick right with me. I, being an only child, needed and longed for my privacy. I thought I would go insane in that tiny dorm room! I was struggling to pass biology and just knew for sure I was going to fail the class. I remember I came home at Thanksgiving break and told my parents that I did not want to go back to ASU after Christmas. I would attend the community college instead. I really wasn't sure what I wanted to do with my life anyway. They were supportive, but I eventually decided that I would stick it out and I learned to like college life. I even passed biology with flying colors – a D plus (or was it a minus?)!

My freshman year I did not take my car to school with me due to the limited parking facilities. I decided to catch a ride back and forth with a fellow who had been a year ahead of me in high school – David. For some reason, my mother always liked this boy. She thought he was so trustworthy because he came from a good family. We became friends on the rides to and from Appalachian. I even had a crush on him at one point, but he was dating someone else.

It seems I was always searching for that special someone who I thought would make me happy. Sadly, I thought my happiness was dependent on someone else. If I didn't have a boyfriend I would become depressed. I don't mean depressed as if I needed medication, but just not happy when I did not have a significant other. I had gotten used to having a boyfriend at a young age. At age fourteen, the beginning of ninth grade, I had started "going with" Mark Long. He and I were practically inseparable. We met at our lockers between classes; we spent our lunch break together when possible; and we sat beside each other in the classes we had together. Mark gave me the first roses I ever received and he asked me to sponsor him on the Homecoming Court in ninth grade. I was even the first girl he ever kissed! Our parents had become friends through our relationship as they sought to get us together on the weekends, taking me to his football and baseball games, hanging out on

Saturday nights, and spending Sunday afternoons at his grandparents' farm. We even went to the beach with each other's families.

Mark and I were truly best friends. We were together for about two and a half years. That's a long time in teenage years! For some reason, sometime during my junior year in high school, I started feeling a little "tied down." Although Mark had done nothing wrong, I thought I was missing out on something exciting. I was only sixteen years old. I think I was afraid I would look back one day and regret not going out with other people and playing the field, so to speak. So, we broke up. It seemed okay at first, until we started actually going out with other people, especially each other's friends. Wow, it really hurt more than I was willing to admit, but we both had too much pride to let our true feelings show. By our senior year, he had met someone from another school and appeared to be serious with her. I had moved on, dating other people, but nothing steady. After all, that was what I had wanted, right?

Mark had received a partial academic/partial baseball scholarship to Lenoir Rhyne College in Hickory, just a short distance down the road from Appalachian. Our paths crossed a few times through our parents' continued get-togethers. I always heard through the grapevine how he was doing and he heard about me as well. However, I think one of us was always dating someone else and our pride was still too huge to overcome. If one of us had taken the first step, we would have possibly faced rejection from the other, and neither of us wanted to take the chance.

My spiritual life, or lack thereof, during college and shortly thereafter was severely beaten down. I often wonder how my life might have turned out if I had earnestly prayed for guidance and truly experienced a relationship with Jesus during that chapter of my life. Instead, I questioned everything I had been taught. I had become close friends with people who had been raised differently from me and been exposed to professors with liberal views. When I did read God's Word, I twisted it to fit my life the way I wanted. Although I believed I was a Christian, I am uncertain of my salvation during this period of my life. I was searching for the wrong things. I thought I needed *someone* to make me happy. I made mistakes that ultimately affected my self-worth. I believe that as a result of my low self-worth, I settled for less than God's best for my life.

The Bible tells us if we're not obedient, God doesn't hear our prayers. **"For the eyes of the Lord are on the righteous and his ears are attentive to their prayer, but the face of the Lord is against those who do evil." 1 Peter 3:12.** I'm afraid I was not in a close enough relationship with Jesus Christ to hear His voice.

In 1992, after graduating from college, I thought the next step should be marriage. The only problem was I didn't even have a boyfriend. All of my apartment mates from college were engaged and getting married within the next year. I had majored in Political Science with a concentration in Paralegal, and minored in Criminal Justice. I was working as a Paralegal Trainee for a law firm in my hometown and was making next to nothing. I really was unhappy with my career choice and was very lonely after I returned home to live with my parents. My friends from high school were no longer around or they had gotten married and were busy with their married lives.

I continued on my search for Mr. Right and even got engaged at one point, then called it off a couple of months later. My love life was a disaster area! I had still not found my perfect job, either. I had left the law firm and gone to work for a large bank. I met a good friend there and we went to the beach together for a weekend in the summer of 1993. We ended up at a nightclub, and who did I run into but David, the nice boy I used to catch a ride with in college who my mother liked so much! But he ended up asking my *friend* to dance!

When we got back home, I would see him while walking at the track at our high school. Sometimes he would be refereeing ballgames. He was a math teacher as well as a coach. One night while hanging around the ball field and track, he asked me out on a date. We started going out, and in October of 1994, after celebrating my acceptance of a new job with the local District Attorney's office, he proposed. We set a date for June 17, 1995.

My mom and I immediately began planning the wedding of the century! I had been going to church with David at his church, so we decided that would be the place where we would get married. My parents had been visiting a large Baptist church for the past couple of years, so I felt "in between" churches. We were planning a pretty big wedding with a reception to follow at a place called the Vintage Theatre. It was to be catered and we had booked a DJ. We were going to have about 7 bridesmaids and groomsmen each. All of my bridesmaids had purchased their dresses. Two of my bridesmaids were his sisters and one was his sister-in-law. Two of his nephews were ring bearers and his niece was the flower girl. She was going to be adorable!

I suppose the reason I am putting so much emphasis on the planning of the wedding is that in my case as in so many others, the premarital counseling with the pastor would happen in the final weeks before the wedding. If there should be any issues, or should there be any second thoughts about the wedding, it would be very difficult to call it off at that point. In our case, we went to counseling with the pastor who was performing the ceremony. We also took premarital classes at the larger church where my parents were attending. Dr. Gary Chapman, author of so many wonderful books on marriage, probably best known for *The Five Love Languages,* taught one of those classes and it was awesome. However, there was one thing that the pastor who performed our ceremony said that I never quite got out of my mind. He said, and this was about a month or two before our big day, "I want you both to pray that if it is not God's will for you two to be married that He would tell you." *Whoa! Wait a second, who did he think he was?* Almost everything had been planned! My parents would kill me if I decided to call it off, wouldn't they? What about the other guy I had gotten engaged to a while back? If I called off a *second* engagement, they might have made a *Runaway Bride* movie about *me!* No one would ever take me seriously again. David and I had also bought a house together, although neither of us was living in it yet. What were we supposed to do about that? However, I think I actually did try to pray that prayer, but my heart really wasn't into it. I think I may have deep down been afraid of the answer. But again, I really wasn't where I needed to be spiritually at this time in my life, and therefore it would have been almost impossible to hear God's voice.

On the day of the wedding, I was so emotional. I went to my grandparents' house to borrow my great grandmother's wedding ring for the "something old and borrowed" and I broke into tears hugging my grandparents. I cried all the way to the church! The borrowed ring did not fit well on my finger as it was a little too loose for my comfort. My matron of honor, Wendy, took her mother's wedding band off her own finger and put it over the ring in order to serve as a ring guard. This too, made me cry because Wendy's mother had been killed in a car accident when we were only three years old. Our moms had been very close friends at the time. As I was getting myself together in the ladies' room, a rosebud arrived from the florist to me from David. The card was handwritten and even his sisters and sister-in-law couldn't believe what a sweet note was written on the card! This seemed to calm my nerves and all was well until the hairdresser had teased my hair and was ready to put the veil on. (This was during my big hair days!) But there was no veil! We had left it at home! I was a basket case all over again! The wife of one of the groomsmen sped back home to retrieve it, and came flying back in the parking lot just in the knick of time! Whew! Then, during the ceremony, I dropped the ring! How comical we all thought these events were afterwards, or could they have served to be little roadblocks from God? Only He knows!

After a really fun wedding reception, we were off to the Cayman Islands where we honeymooned. I adjusted to married life well and tried to be a supportive coach's wife. I was now working for a credit union, and David was coaching at a local high school. We were surrounded by children on both sides of our families. My first cousins, whom I have always been close to, had two young daughters, and David had a precious niece and two really cute nephews. Baby fever soon set in and in the fall of 1996 I became pregnant with our first child the very first month we tried. The first trimester I was very sick. I would throw up almost every time my stomach started to feel empty, and sometimes even when it was full. I was tired all the time! I was soon past that point, though, and enjoyed the remaining pregnancy. On June 25, 1997, our precious daughter, Madison Blair was born. Life would never be the same!

It didn't take long to begin to outgrow the small house we lived in; and in March 1998 we moved to a bigger house in the same neighborhood I grew up in. In fact, we were just down the street from my Grandma Dot and Pap-Paw. David continued to coach and I was working as a processor in the Mortgage

Department at the credit union. Interest rates were low and we were busy. The employees were expected to work overtime and it began to take a toll on my life. My mom had taken a retirement package with the tobacco company as there had been some changes and her job was to be eliminated. God's timing had been perfect in that way as she was able to keep Madison while I worked.

By now I had begun to grow spiritually. We continued to go to the Baptist church and even joined as a family not long after Madison was born. However, no one had ever approached me about being baptized. I knew I was supposed to take the plunge in order to be a member of a Baptist church. I don't know why, but it scared me. I think there was a part of me that had too much pride. I had been raised in the Moravian church and they did not believe in baptism by immersion. I guess at that time in my life I just wasn't ready spiritually because I didn't understand what the big deal was all about. Also, I think I was prideful because it seemed that, if I was baptized at a late age (27ish), people would think I had really sinned in my life. *Duh! Isn't that the point?* Whether we are 7 or 27 we are all sinners! Nonetheless, God was continuing to work on my heart.

During the summer of 1999, we had an interim pastor at our church, Ray Henderson. He was an older, white-haired preacher and I had just fallen in love with him. I really enjoyed his sermons and I was continuing to grow in the Word. While we had never really put forth the effort to go to the Wednesday night services, Pastor was going to do a study on the book of Revelation. David and I were both interested and we took part in the study that summer. I believe I was really feeling the conviction of the Holy Spirit and I was spending more time at home reading my Bible. Something finally clicked inside me and I suddenly had the desire to be baptized. I was still a little nervous about being in front of the entire church, but it was something I knew I needed to do. Our church had voted on a new pastor who would be starting in the fall and I wanted Pastor Ray to baptize me before he left. On June 27, 1999, I finally did it! I remember feeling so great that day after making that profession of faith and I knew in my heart I had been obedient to the Lord.

Fall came and David was again busy coaching football, but I continued going to church on Wednesday evenings. I would take Madison to Mission Friends and I would sit with my father-in-law during prayer meeting. Our new pastor began a study on the book of John. He was a wonderful pastor and I soon grew to love him, too.

In September, I changed jobs within the credit union. I took a position as Team Leader in a new department that had been created. I had escaped the overtime of the Mortgage Department and received a pay raise in the process. Life was good and David and I talked about having more children. We decided we would just see what happened. By this time in my life, I had learned the importance of prayer and spending time with the Lord, but I was still a babe in my faith. I still have the prayer list I used back then. I was praying for people I worked with who were battling cancer, praying for my dad to receive his pension (the plant had closed and he and others he worked with were fighting to receive their full pension), and I was praying that we would have another baby if it was God's will, among other things. Ironically though, I recently ran across that prayer list as I was cleaning and I looked over it. Of all the things I was praying about, my marriage could not be found on the list. Sadly, it had therefore become an easy target for the evil one.

1 Peter 5:8 tells us to **"be self-controlled and alert. Your enemy the devil prowls around like a roaring lion looking**

for someone to devour." During this time in my life, while my faith was being transformed, the enemy was on the move. I can picture a lion, strong and proud with fierce eyes and sharp teeth searching out his next meal, lurking around ever so quietly, and we don't even see him until he's right there in our face! So it was in this circumstance. Looking back I can see we were not on our guard.

Chapter Two

Unanswered Prayers

"And we know that in all things God works for the good of those who love him, who have been called according to his purpose." Romans 8:28

Early one September morning, suspecting I was again with child, I took a pregnancy test before I went to work. Positive! As I told David, a big smile made its way across his face. I felt happy, yet a little scared. I had just started this new position at work and now I was going to have to tell my boss I was going to be going out on maternity leave in a few months. Of course I worried over nothing. She was happy for me and all was well. It didn't take long for the morning sickness (or all day sickness in my case) to set in again. Again, I was fatigued at the end of the day, and felt as if I would be sick all the time. This time it was even harder as I had a two-year-old toddler to take care of in the evenings. My job continued to get more stressful as more work and time-consuming projects were designated to my area.

Our marriage had become strained. We were pulled in different directions with our jobs. David was a teacher and coach at a local high school and was gone quite a bit during football and baseball season. When we were dating and earlier in our marriage, I had been supportive by traveling to both home and away games. Once we had a baby, it became more difficult for me to be as involved in his coaching career.

There were other issues as well that began to creep into our marriage. Our lack of time together combined with a furthered lack of communication and mutual respect and consideration for one another was surely a downfall. We also had major disagreements about what level of friendship was acceptable with a co-worker of the opposite sex. My insecurity and jealousy only sparked my short temper which certainly flared many times during our marriage; none of which I'm proud of. I had a lot of anger because I often felt that my feelings didn't matter as much as others. I'm sure Satan had a field day with us! I certainly was not a perfect wife and have often experienced guilt over the role that I played in the crumbling of our marriage.

Then, after an emotional explosion in January of 2000, it became evident that our marriage was in severe trouble. With much persuasion on my part, we entered counseling with a godly female Christian counselor at my parents' church. Even though we were not members, since we had participated in the premarital classes there and my parents were now members, they graciously agreed to take us on. Our counselor was wonderful to try to help us. She even came in early once a week to meet with us so the sessions didn't cut into David's teaching schedule too badly.

I had shared our problems with our family and a couple of my closest friends but I had not asked for prayer from anyone in our church family, nor had my parents asked anyone in their class to pray for us. Again, my pride got in the way. I didn't want people to talk about us and repeat our problems after we had worked things out. We *had* to work things out! By this time, I was five months pregnant and things were grim, but I prayed we could work things out. By the time I was seven months pregnant, I felt hopeless. I remember our counselor saying to us in one of our meetings, *"Don't become trophies for the devil."* I desperately did not want to end up divorced. I never imagined I would be divorced. I never wanted it to be an option, especially for Madison and for the sake of my unborn child. The thoughts of being a "dysfunctional family" sickened me. I cried all the time, even in my semi-private cubicle at work. It was the worst time in my life.

Out of desperation, I (and my parents) confided in more people as we coveted their prayers. So many people were praying for us! I prayed and prayed that God would change David's heart, and although I had a lot of guilt from my own mistakes, there were many things I did not yet know. I even called Pastor Ray and talked to him. I begged him to come and talk to David, so he agreed to come over one evening. He talked to us and then prayed with us. I remember just crying while he was praying and David was simply unemotional. After Pastor Ray left, I remember waiting for David to say something. I was hoping for some kind of response, but I found none. I felt so helpless.

Finally, as things were revealed to me, (and let me specify that I believe God revealed things to me a little at a time because He knew what was best for me in my pregnant condition), it became evident that our marriage was in fact over. As I came to terms with what was happening, I dropped five pounds in a weekend at seven months pregnant. I was physically sick. I had such a nervous stomach that I literally had vomiting and diarrhea. My doctor threatened to hospitalize me if I lost any more weight. I just didn't have an appetite. I remember just living from one week to the next so I could hear in our counseling session what was on his mind because he certainly wouldn't talk to me. I would repeatedly ask him if he was going to leave me and he would reply that he hadn't decided yet. The tension in our house was becoming too much for me to bear in my pregnant condition. I think he may have been waiting for me to have the baby and then leave me a short time after, so it wouldn't look so bad, leaving a pregnant wife.

Finally, the following weekend, on April 15th, I gave David an ultimatum. I just couldn't go on living in limbo anymore, feeling unloved, especially after some of the things I had learned. He left that day and never returned except to visit the kids and eventually to pick up the rest of his things.

I felt alone and very afraid of my future, but also felt relieved. I was free from the immediate tension that I had experienced while David was living in the house. My appetite began to pick up again and my parents and friends were full of support. I saw the counselor a time or two more on my own and she gave me Dr. Gary Chapman's book *Hope for the Separated*. Life seemed surreal. I think, deep down, I believed that David would soon realize he had made a mistake and come crawling back, but it never happened. I had made an appointment with an attorney and had separation papers drawn up. He would know I was serious. He didn't initially respond to the papers and I was furious.

I began to question why in the world God would allow me to get pregnant if He knew our marriage was going to fail. My very dear friend, Jill, had been trying to get pregnant for some time. She and I would have lunch together almost every day and I would pour out my troubles to her. She is a true friend. Only a true friend would have faithfully listened to me go on the way I did. During this time, she and her husband desperately wanted a baby and even went through the in vitro fertilization process. Unfortunately it was painfully unsuccessful. I wondered why

God had put a baby inside me knowing my husband would leave me, yet He wouldn't bless my friend with a child.

He put **Psalm 139: 13-16** on my heart.

> **"For you created my inmost being; you knit me together in my mother's womb. I praise you because I am fearfully and wonderfully made; your works are wonderful, I know that full well. My frame was not hidden from you when I was made in the secret place. When I was woven together in the depths of the earth, your eyes saw my unformed body.** *All the days ordained for me were written in your book before one of them came to be."* **(Italics mine)**

I began to cling to the fact that God knew exactly what He was doing. This passage not only confirmed that God is the creator of life and He ultimately decides who gets pregnant, but it helped me to understand that God already knew what would happen to my baby and to me. He knew the day I said, *"I do"* that I would face the trouble I was dealing with. He knew the marriage was going to end in divorce and he knew there would be children involved. It was not His perfect plan, but again, I did not allow Him to be involved in my decision for a husband. So, therefore, I do not believe I had His blessing. Our marriage had also not stood up to the attack by the enemy. **Ephesians 6:11-12** tells us:

> **"Put on the full armor of God so that you can take your stand against the devil's schemes. For our struggle is not against flesh and blood, but against the rulers, against the authorities, against the**

powers of this dark world and against the spiritual forces of evil in the heavenly realms."

As Christians we need to be aware of the spiritual warfare that surrounds us. As an immature Christian, I had not been prepared for Satan's attack on my life.

I still couldn't believe what was happening to me. I would lie awake at night and just tremble, my nerves were so bad. I would worry about my baby and wonder if he or she could feel its mommy shaking with fear. I hoped and prayed the baby would be healthy. I would jump up in the middle of the night and run to the bathroom to literally be sick. The nights were so long. I remember just waiting for morning to come. My mom told me I should just ask Jesus to wrap his arms around me as I went to sleep each night, so I did. I really do believe I could feel his presence. My trembling would usually subside as He was letting me know things would be okay.

As I began to tie up all the loose ends on my desk prior to my maternity leave, things became even more stressful. I was afraid someone would find something undone while I was out and then I wouldn't have a job, either. I had never felt so dependent on myself for anything. How was I going to stay in my house on my salary, even with child support? One May evening while I was staying late in the office, I started feeling as though I could be having some light contractions, but I wasn't sure. I decided I had better wrap it up and go to my parents' house. My mom was cooking dinner and I mentioned that I didn't feel quite right. Right away she and my dad told me to call the doctor. Since my appetite was back and I was starving, I said I would call *after* dinner. When I got around to calling, the nurse told me to go on to the hospital. I was in fact having contractions and it was not yet time for the baby to come. I think I was around 32 weeks at this time. The doctor gave me something to stop the contractions and I spent the night in the hospital and the next day or two at my parents' house resting. There was never any explanation for the early contractions except the stress in my life. I just prayed that my baby would be okay. When I did return to work, my mom and dad suggested that Madison and I begin staying with them in case I should go into labor during the night, so I agreed.

I enjoyed being with my parents and didn't feel so alone. My mom, bless her soul, would take Madison and me out almost every night to ride around town and stop by and get a slushy, an ice cream cone, or Krispy Kreme hot glazed doughnuts! It depended on what I was in the mood for! I *did* say my appetite had picked up!

I was, however, becoming more and more frustrated and impatient because my husband had not responded to the separation agreement. I felt like so much was undecided and until we got the legalities worked out, how would I even know if I could stay in my house? I also had a lot of anxiety because I was about to have another child to take care of and I was facing the fact that I was going to be alone. Madison and I could have been okay, just the two of us, but how would I manage with her *and* a baby? How could this really be happening to me? I truly believe I was in some form of denial that I believe most people experience in a separation. It was really hard for me to picture him doing the things I believed he had done, and that he would choose to actually leave his daughter and unborn child. Even if he didn't love me like he once did, shouldn't he want to try to work things out for the sake of our children???

After all those premature labor concerns, it turned out that the baby decided he didn't want to come out when it was time. Ironically, after stopping the premature labor, I later had to be induced. I had gone for my appointment on June 7th and had a stress test. They didn't exactly like what they saw and wanted me to come back and have another one that afternoon. My doctor decided he wanted to induce me the next day. My eyes started filling up with tears as I began to tell him that June 8th was his father's birthday and I didn't want him to be born on his birthday with everything that had transpired. My doctor knew my entire situation and understood, so he told me to go on to the hospital. A different doctor was on call that evening, but I didn't care. My baby was going to have his *own* birthday! All the hospital staff and the employees in my doctor's office were pulling for me to have that baby *before midnight!*

I arrived at the hospital and got hooked up to everything around 5:00 pm. My parents and my cousin, Cindy, were there with me. Cindy's daughter had just had a baby the previous January, and Cindy had taken all the Lamaze classes with her daughter because her daughter's husband was an airline pilot and out of town frequently. Cindy was great! She helped me with my breathing and was a real encourager.

David and his mother and father came to the hospital and were in the waiting room. At one point he walked into the room, but my dad had to go out in order for him to come in. Only three were allowed in the labor and delivery room. I wanted my daddy and I could literally feel my blood pressure go up from the tension in the room when David entered. Cindy must have sensed it, because she asked him to leave and my dad came back in.

Jackson Ray entered the world at 10:40 pm on June 7th...his own birthday!!! I was almost in shock that he was a boy. I had just felt that the baby would be a girl based on its heart rate, which apparently doesn't mean anything. I had actually told a friend of mine that I hoped I would have another girl because I didn't know how to raise a boy as a single mom. I immediately changed my mind when I saw him. I was just amazed that I had a son! I loved him so much! He was named Ray after my grandfather, Ray Pegram. I also thought it was cool that the pastor who had been so influential in my life was named Ray too. I called Madison on the telephone – my grandparents were keeping her while the rest of us were at the hospital. David and his parents came in the delivery room and held Jackson. I don't know if it was the epidural wearing off or my nerves, but I began to shake and I remember telling the nurse I thought I was going to throw up and she brought me a Coke. We were all cordial to one another, but it was very painful for me.

When they took me back to my room, I didn't want to sleep until I could once again hold my baby. My parents came by to say goodnight and then went home. Later that night, actually in the early morning hours, I sat in that hospital bed holding my newborn son. I was just in awe that I had a boy. I was on an emotional high. It was so bittersweet, because I was so happy to have this baby, yet so uncertain of our future and sad for the relationship between me and his father. How could he walk away from us?

I watched him do just that the day we came home from the hospital. He had come to the hospital to see Jackson and Madison, and my mom was there to take us home. I was rolled downstairs in a wheelchair after being discharged and was sitting in the waiting area for my mother to pull the car around. David had walked down with Madison to that point and then I stared at him as he walked to his truck. To my knowledge he never even looked back.

When we arrived home that Friday evening, I remember I was initially in good spirits; walking around outside in the yard carrying Jackson in my arms, talking to the next door neighbors.

I was still on an emotional high…until the telephone rang. It was my attorney and he apologized for calling with the news he had to give me. He had finally heard back from David's lawyer with regard to our separation agreement. The sick feeling in my stomach immediately came back as he told me the changes he wanted to the agreement. I had clung to the hope that certain speculations were not true, but with his response it became crystal clear to me that our marriage was ending. For reasons I couldn't understand at the time, my prayers and those of all the others who had prayed for our marriage became unanswered.

I couldn't understand why God did not answer my prayers to save my marriage, and the prayers of so many others that I knew were praying *for* me. I held onto **Romans 8:28.**

> **"And we know that in all things God works for the good of those who love him, who have been called according to his purpose."**

It *had* to be for my good.

Life Applications for Dealing with a Troubled or Failed Marriage:

1. *Prayer is a vital part of a healthy marriage.* It is never too late to start. There is a spiritual warfare going on all around us and the most effective way to stay on our guard is to pray, pray, pray. In a healthy marriage, it should be a habit to pray for your spouse and even pray *together.* It may be uncomfortable to get started, but there is nothing that binds two hearts like praying together. If your marriage is in trouble, you are more than likely already praying. Be very alert to the devil's schemes and pray in the powerful name of Jesus that He would protect your marriage from future attacks by the enemy. Pray for hearts to soften and change in order to open the door for true healing. If trust has been broken, pray for it to be restored. Remember that it would honor God to show grace to your spouse and He will bless you for staying committed to your marriage vows.

   Key Scripture: **"Be kind and compassionate to one another, forgiving each other, just as in Christ God forgave you." Ephesians 4:32**

2. *Do not be ashamed to ask for prayer from godly prayer warriors.* Intercessory prayer is one of the most effective ways to serve our brothers and sisters in Christ. If you

know a person or persons who can be trusted and are serious in their prayer lives who you would feel comfortable asking to go to the throne on your behalf, then by all means ask them for prayer. There is power in prayer and the more people praying the better! Just be sure that the prayer requests are not a means for gossip, and use discretion in deciding with whom to share your marital problems.

Key Scripture: **"Devote yourselves to prayer, being watchful and thankful." Colossians 4:2**

3. *What happens when you no longer know what to pray?* Sometimes when in a crisis, we are so upset by our circumstances that we just don't know what to pray. We're hurt, we're confused, and we're not sure what we want or what we want God to do in our situation. During these times, we can always simply pray for God's will...whatever that may be. If we are focusing on God and genuinely seeking His will, the Holy Spirit will guide us in our prayers even when we can only cry out in our misery.

Key Scripture: **"In the same way, the Spirit helps us in our weakness. We do not know what we ought to pray for, but the Spirit himself intercedes for us with groans that words cannot express. And he who searches our hearts knows the mind of the Spirit, because the Spirit intercedes for the saints [that's you and me!] in accordance with God's will." Romans 8:26-27**

4. 4. *Accept the outcome...whatever it may be.* This may be the toughest thing for separated/divorced individuals to overcome. So often, just as in a death, we are in a state of denial with regard to our situation. How did this happen? What could I have done differently to have possibly prevented this? For some, it's extremely hard to get on with their lives. They will not allow themselves to get out of the pit they are in due to their circumstances. Have faith that no matter what the devil or anyone else throws at you, God works for your good. When you have reached the point of knowing that you have tried with all your might to fix your marriage, and yet the outcome is not what you had hoped for, *accept it.* There are some things we cannot understand and we should not stay in a miserable, pitiful state for the rest of our lives. That would bring no glory to God! Accept the circumstances and continue serving the Lord. Know with all your heart that He still loves you and will take care of you.

Key Scripture: **"And we know that in all things God works for the good of those who love him, who have been called according to his purpose." Romans 8:28**

Christy Long

Chapter Three

My God, My Great Provider

"And my God will meet all your needs according to his glorious riches in Christ Jesus." Philippians 4:19

That summer while on maternity leave, I spent much of my time on the phone with my attorney or his legal assistant working out the details of the agreement. I was not giving up without a fight. In the end, I think it was a matter of whoever pays the most legal fees wins! But I was satisfied with the outcome. There were two things that were most important for me. First, I didn't want to have to give up time with my children any more than I had to, especially during holidays. Second, I desperately wanted to keep the house. It was just down the street from my grandparents in the neighborhood I grew up in and I also wanted to hold on to it for some sense of security. I didn't want any more changes in our lives for Madison's sake as well as my own. I had gotten down on my knees and turned these burdens over to the Heavenly Father. He was the only one that could handle it for me. He knew my financial situation and He knew what it was going to take for me to keep my house.

I knew that I needed to get rid of my car payment in order to "qualify" to assume our mortgage loan. I had just purchased my Jeep Grand Cherokee in the fall before all this happened and had not even made a year's worth of payments. The only way I knew how to make it work was to withdraw my 401K and take the penalty in order to pay off my car loan. Then it would free up the rest of my income to apply toward the house payment each month among other bills, groceries, etc. Even with child support, it was going to be tight.

My father must have told my Pap-Paw what I had planned to do because he asked me about it one day. I explained my situation to him and he said, *"Don't withdraw your fund, I'll loan you the money at no interest."* The only problem was I didn't know how or when I could pay him back, but I felt that this was God's answer to my prayers. I would be able to stay in my home.

Before he actually gave me the money, Pap-Paw asked me to draw up a promissory note stating how much I owed him and Grandma Dot and for me to sign it. He wanted me to pay Grandma Dot if something were to happen to him. I of course complied with his request. I remember feeling so grateful because this was a big deal for my grandfather. I knew this must have been from God. Only the work of the Holy Spirit could have prompted him to lend me the money interest free. My dad had borrowed money from him in the past, but had always paid him back with interest. My grandparents knew I needed their help, but how would I ever be able to pay them back? I was strapped financially. It was taking every bit of my income to pay the bills and I was still using my credit card for many purchases. I felt as if I was digging myself into a hole.

I should also mention that when I was approved by my mortgage company to assume the loan, the loan officer told me that she had gone out on a limb for me because I didn't meet the criteria for the loan assumption. The reason was that I was not able to provide a year's worth of child support payments in order for that to be counted as income. We had not been separated for a year, only a few months, and the child support amount had just been worked out. Therefore I had not yet received many payments. I thanked her for approving the loan and told her I was good for it! I even saw God at work in Fleet Mortgage!

My parents also provided so much support to me during this time. My mother literally stayed with me for the first four months of Jackson's life. My father was so understanding. He would come over to my house to eat his meals and visit with the grandchildren. My mom told me she wasn't going to go home until Jackson started sleeping through the night. She knew I had to function on my job. I had gone back to work sometime in late July and was slammed with a project as soon as I returned. While the busyness was good in some ways, I still was getting adjusted to having a three-year-old, an infant, and a full-time job. I felt very alone at times, but I was learning to put my trust in God, and although life was a little scary and I was extremely insecure emotionally, I knew somehow things would be all right.

My parents had made sure that the kids and I would get to church on Sunday mornings. My mother would come over and help me get the kids ready and we would go to church together. I knew I needed to get Madison in a Sunday school class, but I was nervous about visiting one myself. There was a singles class that my parents encouraged me to go to. That first morning I visited, my mother literally pushed me through the door. It turned out to be a great thing for me. It was really there in that class where I continued to grow in my faith and be surrounded by other people that had gone through or were going through similar situations.

I felt like a survivor during this time. I didn't have the money to do the things I had been used to doing in life - even simple things like eating out at nice restaurants or buying nice clothes. As an only child, I had enjoyed many of these luxuries and now I was learning what it was like to really watch my money and sometimes do without. I feel I can say, like Paul, that **"I know what it is to be in need, and I know what it is to have plenty. I have learned the secret of being content in any and every situation, whether well fed or hungry, whether living in plenty or in want."** Philippians 4:12 We certainly had enough to eat, but life was very different from what it used to be. As I said, I was using my credit card on a regular basis for clothes for the kids and Christmas presents and was continuing to sink deeper into that financial hole. My checking account also seemed to stay in overdraft mode.

One rainy November morning, I drove to my parents' house to drop the kids off before going to work. My dad was very considerate and would back his vehicle out of the garage on rainy mornings so I could pull inside with my vehicle and unload the children and their things. He had done that on this particular morning. Unfortunately, also on this morning, I was running late for work and had a lot on my mind. I hit the gas as I was backing out of the garage and ran right into his Jeep Cherokee with my own Jeep Grand Cherokee. He later joked and said it was like the demolition derby because I actually knocked his vehicle several feet when I hit it!

Immediately the tears started gushing and I ran back into the house to get some tissue. My precious three-year-old daughter tried to comfort me. She has always been such an encourager! In the end, I had done $3,000.00 worth of damage to our vehicles from that little mishap! Of course I didn't have the money to pay for it, so my car insurance went up as well; again, sinking deeper into the hole.

This was almost too much for me to bear. However, we tried to focus on the fact that no one was hurt and the children were not in the vehicle when it happened. I just felt as if things couldn't get much worse. I worried that I wouldn't be able to pay my grandparents back the money I owed them. I didn't want to let them down and I was afraid that they might be angry or disappointed that I had not made any payments to them.

Even though things were tight financially for me, I tried to be obedient and give the Lord a tenth of what I made. Looking back, I may not have calculated it correctly, but I gave a tenth of my net check – whatever was deposited into my checking account on payday. I had a little going to savings and loan payments before it hit my checking account, so as I said it may not have been a true tithe, but God knew my heart and my intent was to give him the first fruits on payday. Sometimes it was a little hard to write those checks, but I wanted to be faithful to God; He had been so good to me. I was trusting Him to supply all my needs:

"And my God will meet all your needs according to his glorious riches in Christ Jesus." Philippians 4:19

He did provide for me in so many ways during this time. I remember at the credit union where I worked, there was a contest to send in your suggestions for the name of our new employee "intranet" system through which we would receive news, training, and information about our company. My dad has always had a vineyard and therefore the name "Grapevine" came to mind for me – as in "heard it through the grapevine." I actually won the contest and was presented with a $50 gift card to Wal-Mart. An extra $50 was a real blessing to me. When someone asked me what I was going to buy with my $50, I replied, *"Baby formula."* They said, *"Oh, that's so sad!"* It may have been sad, but that was how I could best use that gift card and I was thankful for it!

One Sunday shortly before Christmas, in my Bible fellowship class, a love offering was taken up for a class member who was anonymous. I remember feeling as if there was a real need and when the basket was passed to me, I wanted to give $5, but only had a $10 bill. I didn't feel right taking change out of the basket, but it hurt to give the $10. That kind of puts it in perspective, doesn't it? It was close to Christmas and as a single mom I hated to part with even $10, but I believe the Holy Spirit told me to put it in the basket, so I did.

Christmas was hard for me that year. The kids were with their dad until 6:00 pm on Christmas Eve and that particular day was a Sunday. I had gone to church with my parents and just felt sad all day. My dad came over and helped me put together something for Madison. I don't know what I would have done without him! I remember sort of breaking down as he left my house and he gave me a great big hug and told me things were going to be okay. I just felt so alone and sad. I couldn't wait until 6:00!

That Christmas Eve, as we always did, we celebrated with my Grandma Dot and Pap-Paw at my mom and dad's house. We had dinner and then opened our Christmas presents. After all the presents had been opened, my Pap-Paw slipped me an envelope with my name and Madison's and Jackson's names on it. I really didn't know what to expect. As I opened the envelope and unfolded the paper, I immediately recognized the promissory note I had typed up and signed for them, except on it were the handwritten words "Paid in Full" and my grandparents had written how much they loved us and signed their names! At that moment, I felt such a heavy burden lifted off of me because I just didn't see how I could ever have repaid them. I had felt so overwhelmed with the guilt of not making any payments to them, *but they loved me anyway!* That's exactly what Jesus did for us at the cross when he paid our debt for the sin that we couldn't pay. That's the closest comparison this side of heaven to what Jesus did for me, yet it still cannot even come close to the sacrifice, pain and suffering that He endured on that cross for my sins because of His love for me.

This was nothing short of a Christmas miracle! God was and still is so good to me! But little did I know He had only just begun!

Life Applications for Protecting Your Finances in a Separation/Divorce

1. *Trust God to meet all your needs.* God loves you and He will absolutely meet all of your needs. He is more than capable to supply our daily bread even when the situation seems hopeless. One of my favorite passages of scripture is found in Matthew 6:25-34. In His Sermon on the Mount, Jesus addresses freedom from financial worry. He uses the example of how our heavenly Father feeds the birds of the air and He asks, **"Are you not much more valuable than they?" (v. 26)** Jesus tells us not to worry about what we will eat, drink, or wear because we have a heavenly Father who knows what we need. He goes on to say, **"But seek first his kingdom and his righteousness, and all these things will be given to you as well." (v. 33)** When we put the Lord first in our lives, we can be certain that He will keep His promises to provide for our needs.

    Key Scripture: **"And my God will meet all your needs according to his glorious riches in Christ Jesus." Philippians 4:19**

2. *Avoid digging yourself into a pit of debt.* Going into more debt and sometimes even filing bankruptcy is common during a divorce, because many times one cannot keep up the same standard of living when two incomes are suddenly cut into one. One of the ways a

woman especially can bring financial hardship on herself is by keeping the house during a divorce. A 2005 article entitled "The Five Mistakes Married Women Make" at SmartMoney.com says, *"Too many women fight for the home to avoid uprooting their children, only to find that they don't have the cash flow to pay for it."* The article also states that *"a woman's standard of living decreases by 27% after divorce, according to Richard Peterson, of the Social Science Research Council."* 1 The article recommends getting financial guidance before deciding to take on big payments such as the mortgage. Prayerfully consider this before attempting to take it all on yourself. While your intentions may be admirable for keeping stability for your children, you will be doing them an injustice in the long run if they have to make personal sacrifices as a result of your being between a rock and a hard place financially.

Financial Tips/Questions to Consider:

- Can you afford your mortgage payment, other bills, food expenses, gas, clothing…? If so, will you have anything at all left over to put into savings for when your home needs improvements or new appliances? If you own a home, you probably already know that things break and need to be fixed from time to time. Will you be able to afford it when that happens or will you have to borrow the money?
- You should keep at least 3-6 months of living expenses in a savings account to save for a rainy

day such as a job loss or a major unexpected expense.
- If you receive child support, do not count on your child support payments to automatically increase. Family situations change and typically child support payments do not increase in relation to inflation. I know some women who have never received an increase. Is there room in your budget to adjust to the inflation of the economy?
- Avoid carrying a balance on your credit cards. Make sure you are not using your plastic to live beyond your means. Otherwise, you will never get it paid off and you will continue to sink deeper into financial debt.
- Do not have too much pride. I say this because, for myself, I wanted to give everyone the impression that I was doing just fine. I continued to buy gifts for people at Christmas that I could not afford. I simply put them on the plastic. Perhaps it's going out to lunch or dinner with friends. If you really can't afford it, be honest with them. Your friends and family should understand.
- Develop a budget that works and stick to it. If you do not know how to plan a budget, your local credit union or bank may have the tools on their website to help you establish one for yourself. If not, call your local bank or credit bureau and ask if they offer any free resources for setting up a personal budget. You can always visit your local bookstore for a book written by a

Christian financial planner such as Dave Ramsey or Larry Burkett.
- Before making any purchase, try to ask yourself if this is a *need* or a *want*. There *is* a difference. Be a good steward with what God has given you.

Key Scripture: **"Do not be a man who strikes hands in pledge or puts up security for debts; if you lack the means to pay, your very bed will be snatched from under you." Proverbs 22:26-27**

3. *Give to God first.* God expects us to tithe or give him one-tenth of the first part of our income. I will go more in depth with this concept in a later chapter, but tithing is a part of our obedience to God. It's something He expects from us and we should honor Him by doing so. Even if it seems difficult for us financially, our faithfulness to tithe is a way to show Him that we trust Him.

Key Scripture: **"Honor the Lord with your wealth, with the firstfruits of all your crops;" Proverbs 3:9**

Christy Long

Chapter Four

Security Check

> "One day Naomi her mother-in-law said to her, 'My daughter, should I not try to find a home for you, where you will be well provided for?'"
> Ruth 3:1

Many wise pastors and counselors recommend that one should not date during the separation period. Even though it is "legal", it can oftentimes complicate matters of the heart and obviously hinder any chance of reconciliation between the estranged couple. Having said that, I felt certain that there was no chance of reconciliation in our marriage and I longed to have someone special in my life. I had felt so rejected by my husband for so many months and so very unattractive with my fat pregnant and post-baby body that I wanted to feel desirable again. While I knew my marriage was inevitably over, I hadn't considered just how vulnerable I was when I made the decision to begin dating.

Nevertheless, I ventured into a dating relationship with a fellow I had gone to high school with. He even graduated in the same year as my husband and we had crossed paths a time or two over the last several years. He had never been married, had a good job, and still lived at home with his mother. It actually appealed to me that he had never been married, although my mom told me all along that she almost thought it would be best if I found someone that *had* been married, so they would understand what I had gone through.

I can be thankful that he definitely had commitment issues. Emotionally, I was all over the place during this time. We saw each other, mostly just on Saturday nights, for about 6 months. He treated me well and in a lot of ways helped with my healing process. He took me out to dinner, was good to my children (although he didn't really include them a great deal in activities), and would call me 2-3 times a week. I wanted so much more in a relationship, but he wasn't the guy to give it to me.

As I think back on those few months, I am ashamed that I left my small children with my parents on Saturday nights and wasted precious time worrying over a relationship that was not glorifying to God. You see, he was not a Christian and he had no interest in going with me to church. Satan was continuing to torment me; I was an emotional wreck. I was hanging out with one crowd on Saturday nights and another on Sunday mornings. I had gotten somewhat involved in a Bible Fellowship class at church, but was holding back a little on developing friendships there. People certainly had reached out to me, but I was more interested in pursuing this other relationship. I thought if I remarried, I would get that security back.

Now, don't get me wrong, we never really talked about marriage. He never even told me he loved me and I so desperately wanted to hear it! In fact, I mostly remember staying in emotional turmoil wondering where I stood with this guy. I remember that I had confided in a good friend at work about how I was feeling in the relationship and she told me, *"You know, it shouldn't be this hard. Love is supposed to come easily. I just hate seeing you so stressed out about this guy!"* Ouch! That was the absolute truth. I shouldn't have been wasting so much energy on trying to *make something work*. This was only a dating relationship. Imagine how difficult a marriage would have been.

Satan may have still been bothering me, but I was continuing to grow spiritually at my church. God had not let go of me and the Holy Spirit was most certainly convicting me to focus on my children instead of a man, especially one that wasn't even a Christian.

Finally, one week in March 2001, I was reading my Sunday school lesson and it was titled "Insecurity." Hmmmmm. I still have the quarterly. It begins with this story:

"'I want a divorce.' Her husband's words hit Mary, a woman in her 40s, with the force of a hammer. Her husband of 20 years was abandoning her for a younger woman. Mary had left the work force 15 years earlier to take care of their three children. Where would she live? How would she make a living? These questions flooded her mind and created an overwhelming sense of insecurity."[2]

Wow, did that sound familiar? I had already faced some of these questions. Was I still that insecure? This was speaking right to me.

The lesson was on the Book of Ruth, which is now one of my favorite books of the Bible because I feel like it changed my life. God took care of Ruth and provided for her needs. The lesson focused on how we could trust Him to provide *all* of our needs – physical, emotional, and spiritual. Ruth was a woman of noble character and she was obedient to God. I also loved seeing in Scripture how God used a simple woman like Ruth to carry out a much greater plan. After all, she is even named in the genealogy of Jesus in the Book of Matthew!

It finally clicked for me that God would provide for my *every* need. I had not really trusted Him with the emotional area of my life. I had been trying to make a relationship work that again was not God's best for me. It also became evident to me that in order for God to take care of me and be on my side in life, He expected me to be obedient. Scripture tells us:

> **"If I had cherished sin in my heart, *the Lord would not have listened*; but God has surely listened and heard my voice in prayer." Psalm 66:18-19 (Italics mine)**

I knew that life was too hard and scary to be alone. I most certainly did not want God to turn His back on me. I needed Him to hear my every prayer and meet our needs.

Throughout the Bible, that's the message God sends us. He desires fellowship with His children, but through our sin we are cut off from experiencing that fellowship. He expects us to keep His commands in order for Him to bless us. I don't know about you, but I want to be blessed!

This was most definitely a turning point in my journey. It was surprisingly easy to break up with that fellow I was wasting my time on, and I felt a great deal of peace about it. I knew I had been obedient to the Holy Spirit and there was sweet freedom in that. I began to focus on my children and my church friends as I should have been doing in the first place. I became more active in my Bible Fellowship class at church and even hosted a big spaghetti dinner at my house that spring with kids included. It was a blast, and those friends and activities began to fill the void of loneliness on the weekends.

Let me clarify that the loneliness did not entirely go away. I still had my moments. Later that month, I sent my children, Madison, age three, and Jackson, nine months, to the beach with their dad and his family (and girlfriend, I might add). That was painful for me. His oldest niece was getting married and although he wasn't supposed to have Jackson overnight until he was one year old, I agreed to let him go because I knew it meant a lot to his parents to have all the family together at the wedding. I kept busy that weekend and prayed like crazy.

The next couple of months were pretty low key for me. I did go out with a couple of guys from church, but just had feelings of friendship for them. I finally felt that I could distinguish the difference between having real feelings for someone vs. being in love with being "in love." I wasn't going to settle for less than God's best for me this time. I wouldn't soon forget about Ruth.

Christy Long

Life Applications for Dealing with Insecurity

Determining when You're Ready to Date Again

When is it okay to date again? This is a very common question that you may be asking yourself after a separation/divorce. Some say that you should not date until you are actually divorced; some say it is okay after you are "legally separated." I have even heard one pastor recommend not dating again until it has been *two years* after a divorce. That of course is because of the vulnerability of your heart during those first two years; it sets a boundary for not jumping into another relationship or even *marriage* before your heart is ready. Ultimately, it is up to the individual. Here are a few suggestions to ponder before making the dating decision.

1. *Make sure you're placing your security in the only One who can give it.* Focus on your relationship with Jesus and seek Him for providing any security of which you are in need. Remember, He will meet all your needs (Philippians 4:19)
2. *Pray, pray, pray.* Ask the Holy Spirit to guide you and lead you in making the decision to date again so that you'll know when the time is right.
3. *Make the choice to be happy and content where you are in life before entering into another relationship.* Do not expect to find happiness or completeness in another person. Only Jesus can provide the completeness or wholeness our souls crave. If you have children, focus

on raising them. They will be grown before you know it and you will never get that time back. Find a good group of other Christian singles to do things with, but be cautious. Others may be vulnerable as well and they may be looking to *you* for happiness instead of Christ. If you become involved in a singles group, I recommend getting to know someone as a friend for at least six months before even considering going out on a date with him. That gives each of you enough time to sort out your feelings and make sure you're not simply just in love with being in love again. It will also give you enough time to make sure that he is not just interested in the next cute, hot "thang" to come to church. This may sound bad, but unfortunately there are people who just go to church to find a mate. Once you have established these boundaries, proceed with caution.
4. *If you have children, make sure to guard their hearts.* More than likely, they have already been through enough. Be considerate of their feelings. It is not wise to introduce lots of possible significant others to them. Wait until a relationship has gotten past the initial "getting to know you better" stage before possibly confusing your kids. You do not want to cause them to feel resentful about a new relationship or maybe even get their hopes up and break their heart(s) if the relationship ends.
5. *Remember to honor God with any relationship.* Stay in the Word and be alert. Do not ignore any "red flags" in the relationship simply because you may be feeling lonely. For **"If we claim to have fellowship with Him yet walk in darkness, we lie and do not live by the truth." 1 John 1:6** Although we human beings do make

mistakes, take note if a new love interest talks the talk, but doesn't walk the walk. Also remember that because this is a vulnerable time, you may experience temptation. God's Word tells us to flee from sexual immorality (See 1 Corinthians 6:18), but the good news is that He will not let us be tempted beyond what we can bear. Furthermore, He will also provide a way out for us. (See 1 Corinthians 10:13)

Key Scripture: **"Do not be yoked together with unbelievers. For what do righteousness and wickedness have in common? Or what fellowship can light have with darkness?" 2 Corinthians 6:14**

Chapter Five

Hope and a Future

"'For I know the plans I have for you,' declares the Lord, 'plans to prosper you and not to harm you, plans to give you hope and a future.'"
Jeremiah 29:11

"Blue Skies" was exactly what I experienced at Cherry Grove Beach, South Carolina, in June 2001. I loved that song by Point of Grace and it played frequently on the radio that summer. It was a gorgeous and perfect beach week and I was thrilled to be spending it with my parents and precious children at the oceanfront condo we rented, with a big screened-in porch with a swing and rockers. Jackson had just turned one year old the week before and he was walking. He looked like a tiny, little man as he walked along the shore pointing up in the sky at the open cockpit yellow airplane that would fly above the coastline.

This was the first time I ever remember going to the beach and taking my Bible. I had been doing a Bible study on the Book of Daniel with my Singles Bible Fellowship class that summer and I took my Bible so that I could work on that as well as to just have my quiet time each day. My parents also had their Bibles and spent time in the Word as well. One morning my dad said, *"I thought about you when I read this verse."* He showed me a passage in Psalms.

> "Though you have made me see troubles, many and bitter, you will restore my life again, from the depths of the earth you will again bring me up." Psalm 71:20

That was so promising to me that even though I had been through some tough times over the last year or so and I had become a single mom raising two small kids, God was going to restore my life again. He would bring me up out of the pit that I had found myself in.

I continued to believe Romans 8:28 that He was working things out for my good and I knew that He had plans for me.

> "'For I know the plans I have for you,' declares the Lord, 'plans to prosper you and not to harm you, plans to give you hope and a future. Then you will call upon me and come and pray to me, and I will listen to you. You will seek me and find me when you seek me with all your heart.'" Jeremiah 29:11-13

During that week, after spending quite a bit of time in the Word, I went for long walks on the beach. I would talk to God as I walked. I distinctly remember on one of those walks telling God that *I would really love to find someone to spend the rest of my life with and I was asking Him to lead me to that person, someone I would be evenly yoked with.* Paul tells us in **2 Corinthians 6:14, "Do not be yoked together with unbelievers..."** I had learned the importance of choosing a mate who had the same spiritual beliefs that I had, and yet I knew how difficult it seemed that there would be anyone left out there in this great big world in my age bracket, much less my "spiritual" bracket that would be "available" and even further, that I would actually feel attracted to! So I went on to pray, *Lord, if there isn't anyone out there, that's okay too...just help me to raise my kids alone and focus on them.* I was prepared to accept whatever His will was for my life with or without a "soul mate." I had finally reached the point in my life that GOD WAS ENOUGH.

As we drove home from the beach the following Saturday, I felt refreshed. I also remember my mother saying to me that the Longs were on their way to the beach that day. The Longs, as in Mark Long, my first real boyfriend. Our families had kept in touch through the years. I had only seen him two or three times over the last five years or so. He and his fiancée attended my wedding; less than two months later, David and I and my parents and in-laws went to his wedding. I also saw him and his wife at our ten-year high school class reunion in 1998. He was there to help Madison up when she fell and cut her lip in the parking lot. We saw him again at his sister's wedding in 1999, where he offered to let me use his cell phone to call and check on Madison. I had even run into him that past fall at a college football game while he was in town working on his sales job. I was with some friends, including one of my girlfriends from high school, and we had giggled that we saw my "old boyfriend." After all, he was then married and living in Charlotte. However, he had taken a job in our hometown. It was simply by chance that we saw each other and briefly said "hello." *We had thought, What are the odds of running into him?*

Later that year, his wife had left him and our circumstances were so similar – he just wasn't pregnant! At this point, his wife had been gone for several months and they were legally separated. I had not made any attempt to contact him because I didn't know if there was any chance of their reconciling, and I did not want to interfere with that, nor did I want to hurt him again. However, I did pray for him. I recently ran across an old prayer list that I was carrying around during that time and I had prayed first, that he and his wife would work things out if it were God's will, and second, I prayed for healing. After all, I had been through the same situation and had experienced some of the same hurt about six months ahead of him. I remember thinking about him often and wondered how he was doing, but I did not dare call him.

After my renewed beach trip, things got back to normal, though I will not say that I was never lonely again. My divorce was final on June 25, 2001 – Madison's fourth birthday. It was a day of mixed emotions. There was sadness because I reminisced back to the same date four years earlier when we were at the hospital having our first baby. I never would have thought that four years later our names would be called in Divorce Court and our marriage would cease to exist. It almost felt like a death, and it was in a way. There was also a feeling of closure. I was a free woman, but truthfully that didn't make me feel so great.

I specifically remember one Sunday afternoon feeling extremely "blue." My children were with their dad for a couple of days and I should have welcomed a quiet time of relaxation, but instead I longed for someone special to spend time with. That evening as I went to bed, the movie *An Officer and a Gentleman* was on TV. As I continued to watch the happy ending, the old song "Up Where We Belong" began to play. As silly as it sounds, I couldn't help thinking about the eighth grade dance in junior high school when Mark and I slow danced to this song after our friends had literally pushed us together because they knew we liked each other! Again, I thought of him and wondered how he was doing.

A short time later, my mom called to check in on me. She said, *"I just called to talk to Jan Long (Mark's mother) and you'll never guess who I talked to."* She went on to tell me that Mark was spending the night with them because he had an early meeting on Monday morning and he answered the phone and they chatted for a minute. I said, *"I wonder how he's doing?"* My mom said, *"I don't know, why don't you call and talk to him?"* I'll never forget the words that came out of my mouth, *"No, he knows how to reach me if he wants to talk to me."* I was very determined that I would not be the one to make any kind of a move. I still didn't want to interfere in any way and I definitely did not want to hurt him. I realized that I had not really been around him much at all in the last few years and I didn't even know if I would feel the same way about him that I used to all those years ago. We were just kids then.

The next morning as I was driving up Highway 52 to work, another old eighties song came on the radio. This time, it brought a smile to my face because it was "our song" back in that day. "You're the Inspiration" by Chicago is not so often heard on the radio anymore and yet here it was, playing a coincidentally, cheerful melody on this bright, sunny July morning – with *blue skies* I might add! But again, I dismissed the thought. *He can call me*, I affirmed to myself.

The next afternoon was July 3rd and since it was the day before a holiday I had asked to leave a little early because I needed to go by the DMV and change my name on my driver's license. I had decided to take my maiden name back, since my ex-husband was dating a "Christy." I had worked in the lending industry long enough to know how complicated a credit report could get when two women with the same name were married to the same man! *Didn't want to go there!* As I was packing up my things in my cubicle, our IT Manager came over to me and asked that I step in his office. He was a kind, father figure type who had checked on me from time to time at the office and had given me the constant advice of, *"Take the high road,"* throughout my separation battle with my ex-husband, but I had no idea what he wanted to show me. He motioned for me to look at the email on his computer. Then, he asked me if I knew a *"Mark Long."* As I began to read the email, I started laughing with excitement. Then I turned red with embarrassment after I realized that I must have been acting like a teenager. He just sat back in his chair and grinned at me as if he enjoyed watching me act like a silly school girl. I exclaimed, *"He's my old boyfriend from high school!"*

Mark worked for a local company that handled the computer server for the credit union. He was able to come up with my email address, but he had typed it backwards and therefore, the email defaulted to the IT Manager. The whole thing was very comical. He printed the email for me and I read it over and over. Mark was basically just sending me a friendly email catching up, but I felt in my heart that he was interested in seeing me. Unfortunately, I couldn't respond to him because I had to get to that long line at the DMV. Just knowing that Mark had contacted me made the wait go faster.

Later that evening, I pondered whether or not I should just try to call him because I didn't have email access at home and the next day was the Fourth of July. I wouldn't be at work to respond to his email. The last thing I wanted was for him to think that I didn't reply to his email. So after much consideration, I picked up the phone and called his mother. I'm not sure what she thought because I'm sure she had no idea that her son had made contact with me, but I explained that I had gotten an email from him and I thought I would just pick up the phone and call him instead. She said, *"Yes, Bell South works just as well, doesn't it?"* I finally worked up my nerve to call him that night from my parents' house and he wasn't home. Then, when I got home, he had left me a message on *my* machine! We were playing phone tag! Finally, we spoke on the phone later that night. It was good to hear his voice again. Then he said, *"Let's grab some dinner one night next week and catch up!"* So we made plans for Monday night.

God's timing is always perfect! My kids left for the beach with their dad and his family the Saturday after the Fourth of July. I had been dreading that trip for months. My children were so young, Madison, four, and Jackson, one. I worried about them playing in the water, being on the highway, just their general well-being for an entire week away from their mother. This would be the first of many one-week beach trips in which I would miss them like crazy, but God had a plan to keep me busy this week. I thought it was interesting that my children were staying at a place called the Sea Mark, and I was going to *see Mark*! He knew I would need a little excitement in my life to get me through and He was faithful to provide just that!

I told myself that I would not get too excited about this "date" with Mark. I wasn't even sure it *was* a date. We were just two old friends getting together for dinner to "catch up." Even if there was no physical attraction there, I would be his friend and he could be mine. After all, it would be nice to have a friend.

From the moment Mark came to the door to pick me up that Monday evening, it was just like being with an old familiar friend. The only difference was I found that I *was* still attracted to him after all those years. He took me to dinner at a nice restaurant with patio seating and we enjoyed the warm summer evening. We stayed there for hours it seemed, just talking and talking. It was so amazing how very similar our circumstances had been in the failure of our marriages. There was a great deal of comfort in being able to share those feelings with someone who knew exactly where you were coming from. He expressed to me that his wife had moved on and the damage was so great that there was absolutely no chance of reconciliation. I could certainly relate to what he said based on what had happened in my own situation. (In retrospect, it may have been more prudent to have strictly remained friends until his divorce was final, but I do not believe the outcome would have been any different.)

We went back to my house and continued talking until around 1:00 in the morning – we both had to go to work the next day and he had to drive back to Charlotte! My mom even called really late to see how it went, and *he was still there*! We also talked a great deal about spiritual things and shared things in our faith. At one point, we even had my Bible on the floor of my living room trying to find a particular passage of Scripture. Mark had read something that said whatever the devil stole from us, God would repay it to us *sevenfold!* Although neither of us is blameless and far from perfect, in both of our failed marriages, we were the ones that had tried to save them. We both felt the enemy had stolen from us, but we had faith that God would make it right. *"Double for your Trouble"* is a popular phrase that several Christian pastors and speakers have used to describe **Isaiah 61:7**:

> **"Instead of their shame my people will receive a *double portion*, and instead of disgrace they will rejoice in their inheritance; and so they will inherit a *double portion* in their land, and everlasting joy will be theirs. (Italics mine)**

I had certainly felt shame and disgrace over my situation - a failed marriage, with a toddler and an unborn baby. I knew people felt sorry for me and I hated that feeling, but God wasn't finished working. My life was not yet over. I was putting my trust in the Lord. Would He really restore *double* what I had lost?

It quickly became evident to me that even though Mark and I had taken different paths through the last fifteen or so years, God had led us back together; and that we actually seemed to be spiritually yoked with each other. Funny, in our teens we never talked much about spiritual things. We both went to church, but neither of us had really experienced the salvation of Jesus Christ back then. Now it was apparent that we had each grown spiritually and it came so naturally to discuss such things.

As the week went on, we had lunch together several times. He would pull up in front of my office building downtown to pick me up and would actually get out of his white Chevrolet truck and walk around and open the door for me to get in. He was such a gentleman – he was like my Prince Charming except instead of riding a white horse, he was driving a white pick-up! He knew that I loved my coffee and he brought me a bag of Starbucks. This was a real treat because these were the days before our city was blessed with a Starbucks on every corner. I smelled the aroma as soon as I stepped inside the vehicle. Mmmmm! He also brought a book for me to borrow. It was a double novel by Frank Peretti, *This Present Darkness* and *Piercing the Darkness*. We had discussed the presence of the enemy and how spiritual warfare was very real. Mark had recommended those books, so he brought them to me to read. He was so thoughtful.

I was a little bummed because he was involved in a business that had a quarterly out-of-town meeting the next weekend, so we were not going to be able to see each other. He hadn't yet met my children and they were coming home from the beach on Saturday. It was so wonderful to get them home. I had missed them so much, but again God had chosen *that* week to bring Mark back into my life and keep me busy and happy.

Early next week, Mark came over to meet the children. Madison and Jackson walked over to the front door and peeked out the windows on each side to check him out as he walked up the front steps. I told them he was Mommy's friend from high school. Madison and Jackson immediately befriended him. He was so good with them. He always included them in whatever we did and never made me feel like I had "baggage," as some people might have done.

It didn't take long for Mark to pose the question in email form one day after one of our lunch dates, *"What did I think about all of this?"* He basically was asking me where he stood. I thought long and hard about it before I replied. I remember telling him that it felt like a new, exciting relationship, yet there was an old comfortable feeling because of the past we had shared. It was so easy to fall right back into love with him all over again.

After a couple of months, he decided that it didn't make sense to stay in Charlotte anymore since his job and his family were here. He began looking for an apartment and again God's timing was perfect. We live in a rural area in our county and apartments or duplexes are hard to come by. It just so happened that some duplexes were just being finished exactly halfway between my house and his parents' house. He called the number on the rental sign and he was able to rent the *last unit available*. Nothing could be more perfect!

Throughout the next year, we saw each other almost every night, had many lunch dates, and he began going with me to church, where he soon joined. I knew God meant for us to be together. On June 15, 2002, at Surfside Beach, South Carolina while on vacation with his family and my kids, Mark and I went for a late night walk on the beach. We walked and walked and walked and walked. I thought he was acting a little strange and he kept one hand in his pocket the whole time. We started talking about how we had been brought back together and about our dreams. I remember he said something very profound about the waves washing up on the beach and washing away the sand, the way God washes away our mistakes so we can start fresh again. I thought that was such a beautiful analogy and I still think about it when I walk along the beach. I was, however, starting to get a little suspicious when finally Mark took my hand, dropped to his knees and asked, *"Will you marry me?"* Of course I said, *"YES!"*

All of our families and even two other families we were friends with were vacationing together at Surfside that week. When we walked out on the beach the next morning, they all started applauding! These were our friends from back in the old days and they knew our history and what we had gone through. Everyone was truly happy for us.

We began planning the wedding immediately and decided on a date of October 19th. Since Mark and I had both taken on the marital debt from our first marriages, we really didn't have a lot of money to take an extravagant honeymoon, nor did I want to leave the kids for very long because they were so young. Madison would be five and Jackson two. We even talked about eloping since this was our second wedding, but I wanted my children to be included in the ceremony and Mark agreed. We both love Civil War history and the whole aura of the Old South, so we decided we would stay at a bed and breakfast in Charleston, South Carolina for a few days.

While we were still at the beach, I had, of course, called my grandparents to tell them the news. They happened to be at my cousin Cindy's house for Father's Day and my entire extended family was thrilled for us. Cindy was the cousin that was by my side when I gave birth to Jackson just two years prior. She and her husband have a gorgeous old home in a prominent, historical area of the city. Their home is fabulous for entertaining and decorated like something out of *Southern Living*. At that time she was in the Rose Society and had an absolutely immaculate rose garden. She has a beautiful, covered side porch that overlooks the garden. When she heard the news, she insisted that we get married at their home! At first I wasn't sure about it, but she really wanted to do that for us and I knew if she planned it, it would be elegant!

We kept the guest list quite small, just our immediate family and two or three families that we were close to throughout the years. Mark and I went to premarital classes at our church and since we had also been going to the Wednesday night service when Pastor Todd Phillips preached, we decided we would ask him to perform our marriage ceremony. Todd knew my situation, but really didn't know Mark that well yet. We met with him at least twice before he agreed to do our wedding. He said he had never done a wedding where both the bride *and* the groom had been divorced. He wanted to hear what happened in our first marriages before he would decide to marry us, so we complied with his request and he agreed to do it. Mark later played on Todd's softball team at church and they became friends.

Again, on October 19th there were *blue skies* and it was a warm fall day. Madison was a precious flower girl and Jackson was a handsome ring bearer. He walked with my mother down the outdoor "aisle" under the arbors and around to the porch. Madison followed dropping the rose petals on the ground. Then my dad gave me away a *second* time. A friend from my Singles

Bible Fellowship class played the guitar. It was very small, intimate and special. I was much more emotional this time around. It was all I could do to hold back the tears. Then during the ceremony, Mark gave Madison and Jackson their special wedding gifts. He had purchased a gold cross necklace for Madison and a gold cross lapel pin for Jackson. We couldn't really hear what he was saying to them, but knew that he was "marrying" them as well by promising to love them and be their step-dad.

After the ceremony and before dinner, my dad prayed the most beautiful blessing not only for the delicious food, but for our marriage. While I don't remember all of his exact words, he said, *"An hour ago there were three and now there are four."* We were a family of four. God had been so FAITHFUL and so GOOD to me. He had brought true love back into my life and worked all things for our good.

We spent the first night of our honeymoon at Harmony House Bed and Breakfast in Rock Hill, South Carolina, then went on to Charleston the next day. We stayed at the Governor's House Inn in the historical district and enjoyed all the mouth watering low-country cuisine. We had breakfast on the veranda each morning and sipped afternoon tea later in the day. We enjoyed taking in all the sights and of course each other's company. I did miss my children and I know they missed their mommy. The night we came back home, they were thrilled to see us. Madison was walking under the garage door looking for me with excitement as it was rising. That night, all four of us got into our big king size bed and slept together. We were all together, happy and content.

Christy Long

Life Applications for Believing that God Will Give You Hope and a Future

1. *Look to God for your hope and future.* Remember that our God is like "blue skies." He is our light and He is always there. Sometimes during our storms of life we can't see Him through the clouds and the rain because they block out His radiant sunshine, but He never leaves us. Just as the clouds part after the rain, He brings us blue skies again. The storms only last *for a little while*.

   Key Scripture: **"And the God of all grace, who called you to his eternal glory in Christ, after you have *suffered a little while*, will himself restore you and make you strong, firm and steadfast."** 1 Peter 5:10 **(Italics mine)**

2. *Submit to His will for your life so He can accomplish His plan.* There is really not much to say about this one. We simply need to cooperate with God by submitting to His will. If we keep trying to do it ourselves and make our own plans happen, we will interfere with His *best* plan for us and miss out!

   Key Scripture: **"'For you know the plans I have for you', declares the Lord, 'plans to prosper you and not to harm you, plans to give you hope and a future. Then you will call upon me and come and pray to me, and I will listen to you. You will seek me and find** me when you seek me with all your heart.'" **Jeremiah 29:11-13**

3. *Believe He will do what He says He will do.* God is faithful. He keeps His promises. Our part is to have faith and believe Him for what His Word says.

Key Scripture: **"Now faith is being sure of what we hope for and certain of what we do not see." Hebrews 11:1**

God Keeps His Promises

Just the Three of Us

Pegram Family Portrait

My First Roses on My Birthday (from Mark), August, 1985

Our Wedding Day - October 19, 2002

God Keeps His Promises

New Family of Four - (our wedding portrait)
Photo by Dalton Photography 2002

Happy Father's Day from newborn Bryson!
June 18, 2006

Our Family in Maui, 2007 - Aloha!

Christy Long

Chapter Six

Been There, Done That

> "For the Lord is good and his love endures forever; his faithfulness continues through all generations."
> Psalm 100:5

It certainly didn't take long to get back to the reality of life. Madison was in kindergarten, and Jackson stayed with my parents during the day. Mornings were rushed as I dropped her off at school, then made a stop at my parents' house with Jackson and all of his things. Work was still busy with more work to do than people to do it and I was given another project soon after that consumed a lot of time. Mark's job in software sales demanded long hours as well as traveling, but we were adjusting to married life well.

About four months after we were married and after some concern about the viability of the company Mark was working for, I answered the phone one day at work to hear his voice on the other end saying, *"Well, this ride is over, they're laying off all the sales people."* The company filed Chapter 11 Bankruptcy and many were left without their jobs and their stock. I assured Mark that things would be okay and he would find another job soon. I knew God would meet our needs. I had already been through a tough time in my own life and He had taken care of my children and me. I knew He would provide again. Because of His faithfulness and goodness He had already shown, I was not terribly worried about our situation. We were also living in the house that I had before we were married and I was able to make the house payments and the regular bills with my income. Mark did, however, have a car payment and a couple of credit card bills that wouldn't be easy for me to take on. We would have to rely on our savings to make those payments until he could find something else.

He was out of work for approximately two months. I know it must have been hard for him emotionally because he, as a male, wanted to take on the role of provider and especially being newly married, this was not a good thing to happen. I think it was an opportunity for us to trust the Lord and to grow stronger as a couple. Mark and I have both been used to "having things," sometimes whether we could really afford them or not. One can afford just about anything nowadays with plastic and unfortunately that was the world we had lived in. He had admitted to me that in his first marriage they had lived beyond their means and I knew he had the credit card bills to prove it. We had both accumulated the marital debts from our previous lives and truthfully, at times I felt resentful. We learned that there were many things we did not *really need* to have. If we had to use a credit card to purchase it, we probably *shouldn't* purchase it. Through his job loss, saving for a rainy day became a priority for us and we vowed to pay off that credit card debt.

He took a job with another company, which he hated. I felt bad for him, but he needed the job. It was again in sales but he did not have as much freedom as he was used to; he had to wear a tie every day; and actually had to learn to be punctual! Now don't get me wrong; my husband is a very hard worker. He is always working at home early in the morning and late into the night, and therefore no one minds if he is not walking in the door to the office at a set time each day. However, in this job he was expected to work a set number of hours *in* the office, and he *was* expected to be on time. Not to mention the fact that he had to spend three weeks in Phoenix, Arizona for training the first three months of his employment – one week during each of the first three months. I was not happy about that either, but again, he needed the work.

The second week he was in Phoenix, his grandmother, whom he was extremely close to, passed away. She was in the hospital when he left town, but he had to leave for the training. Although her health had severely declined, her death was somewhat of a surprise to us. She and his grandfather, who had passed away some twelve years earlier, lived up the road from Mark when he was growing up. He used to play on the farm and later work on the farm with his grandpa. His grandma was a wonderful cook and friend to Mark. She loved her grandson and it has even been said that she thought he was perfect – or at least as perfect as one *can be*! Mark was unfortunately all alone upon hearing the news and of course had to fly home early.

He was scheduled to go back to Phoenix the next month, but he had another job offer on the table by then. We were at the beach with Mark's family when he made the decision. It was a huge decision. This seemed to be quite an opportunity – the first salesperson hired for a new software company – the entire southeastern United States as the territory – opportunity for advancement – great commission plan... The problem? It was a company started by the same people that had owned the previous company he had worked for that had filed bankruptcy. He was going to be working for the same people that laid him off in the first place. Was this really a good idea? We prayed about it and prayed about it some more. Finally, it became evident that it was a real opportunity and if he lost his job again, then he would find another one *again*. After all, he was miserable in his current situation *and he wouldn't have to go to Phoenix again!* He took the job and has been with the company for about five years now. It has been one of the best decisions he ever made. If it falls apart tomorrow, the Lord has definitely used this company to provide for our family over the past five years and we are thankful to the One who opened that door!

In the fall of 2003, we started talking about trying to have a baby. It seemed to us like a good time to expand our family. Mark's mom had planned a trip to Disney World for our family and we were so looking forward to going! I had not been to Disney since I was a kid and, therefore, wanted to ride all the new thrilling rides at all the theme parks. We decided that we would start trying *after* our trip.

We did try for a couple of months, and I was disappointed because I didn't get pregnant right away. Meanwhile, at my yearly OB/GYN visit, the PA discovered a lump in my breast. I had felt it also and became alarmed at the way she just sort of froze when she ran across it. She wanted to see me again the next month, then again the next. Then, she sent me for a mammogram and an ultrasound to be on the safe side. While going through all of these tests, Mark and I decided that maybe we would just stop trying for the time being to have a baby just in case there was something physically wrong with me. I was anxious and a little angry because I wanted answers. I couldn't understand why the doctors were dragging out these tests. It turned out to be nothing, but I believe the Lord used that to keep us from having a child at that time. He knew it was *not* the right time, as we would soon find out.

Mark and I had begun to discuss the possibility of moving into a larger house since we had been talking about having another child. Even if we didn't have another baby, we were outgrowing our space. He had converted the kids' toy room into an office and the kids' bedrooms were so small they had nowhere to put their toys. They were in a mountain in the corner of our living room, which wasn't very big. We had looked around at open houses in our area, but what we really wanted was to fix up Mark's grandparents' house. It had been sitting since his grandmother passed away the previous spring and we didn't know what the family planned to do with it. Mark loved that place and I also had fond memories of hanging out there on Sunday afternoons back in our young high school days. It had a big front porch with a swing on each end and we would sometimes just go over there and sit and let the kids play in the yard. He continued to help out with cutting wood on the land around the farm. It was a house with 59 acres and we couldn't afford to buy that amount of land. It belonged to Mark's dad and Mark's uncle, equally. I could envision so much with the house. It could be beautiful again – it needed so much work, though! We knew that we couldn't afford to spend a great deal of money purchasing the house and then spend even more to fix it up like we wanted. Mark had let his family know that we wouldn't mind living there and fixing the place up, but that was all. There had been no discussion of the selling price, so we just waited and prayed for an answer.

    Unexpectedly, one Sunday afternoon, as I was sitting on the floor wrapping Christmas presents, Mark came home after being over at the farm and said, *"Okay, here's the deal...They're going to give us the house and an acre...as long as my uncle can come over and play with his tractor when he wants to."* I was really happily shocked and immediately started crying. This was again an answered prayer, because we truly wanted to fix the place up and live there and of course once again God had not only provided, but had given more than we could have even imagined. We couldn't believe they were giving it to us! We were so thrilled! We would be able to make it our dream house!

The spring of 2004 was very busy for us. Mark and his mother spent many hours demolishing most of the inside of the house. It was mostly gutted inside, except for the living room which would become our study. We kept the knotty pine paneling on the walls and there is something old and familiar about that room which we love. We added on to each end of the house as well as upstairs. It would be much like the old home place – white siding with black shutters; and, of course, we were keeping the porch with the two swings on each end! Mark spent a lot of time working on the house as did his mom because there were so many of his grandparents' belongings still inside that needed to be sorted. We found a builder and began the whole process of viewing other homes and selecting materials.

My grandmother, "Grandma Dot", began kidney dialysis that year and her health was rapidly declining. She was admitted to the hospital in April and it was becoming apparent to my Pap-Paw that he was going to have to make some tough decisions concerning her care. The Lord made those decisions for him because He decided to take her home on the morning of April 26th. We had just visited with her in the hospital the afternoon before. I had been so busy trying to get ready to put our house on the market. I had planted flowers on Saturday that weekend and then went by for a quick visit on Saturday night, then dropped in on Sunday after church for a while. I had planned to take a day of vacation on Monday and told her I would be back over to see her then and I would stay longer. I never got the chance because she died shortly after 6:00 that morning from cardiac arrest. I was almost hysterical and in disbelief when I awoke to the news on the phone that my Grandma Dot was gone. How I would have loved to have had just one more day with her! I was angry with myself and immediately felt guilty for not spending more time with her over the weekend. We won't always have tomorrow.

I was thankful, however, that a couple of weeks before her death, Mark and I had taken my grandparents down to our house in its original state. It was a beautiful spring day and Grandma Dot had enjoyed sitting in one of the front porch swings, while we showed Pap-Paw around the house and told him the changes and additions we were planning to make. Then we all sat on the porch and visited for a little while.

We put our house on the market later that spring. We knew we would need every penny of equity we had in our current home to apply to our new home. We just really didn't have any idea just how badly at this point! We put a "For Sale by Owner" sign in the yard and I hung flyers at the restaurants and grocery stores in our area. We even ran an ad in the newspaper and held an open house on a hot summer Sunday. We really didn't want to have to pay a realtor's six percent commission if we didn't have to. We were praying that if it was God's will, we would sell it on our own – that He would send just the right buyer at the right time. In fact, we thought we had it sold rather quickly. There was a young couple that came to see the house and offered us full asking price on the spot! However, if that offer seemed too good to be true, it's because it was! After having our attorney prepare a contract for the deal, the couple never signed it nor did they ever write us an earnest money check. It became very frustrating because she assured me they wanted the house, but they needed to sell their house first. I believe they may have received some criticism from their family for offering us full price as well and they may have been embarrassed for jumping so quickly.

The summer went on and while we showed our house several times, we still didn't have an offer on the table. Our new house was scheduled to be completed in October, so we agreed that we would try to sell our house "For Sale by Owner" through August. After that, we would just go ahead and list it with a realtor. We couldn't afford two house payments. I remember one August morning in Sunday school during Prayer and Praise, I said, *"We really need to sell our house."* I have no doubt our brothers and sisters in Christ were praying for us! On August 31st around 10:00 that night, I received a call from a fellow about our house. He had been driving around and had seen our sign. He asked if he and his wife could look at it the following night. At that time, I helped teach Mission Friends at church on Wednesday evenings, so I told him we could do it around 8:00 if that wasn't too late.

The next evening the couple showed up with their little boy and the wife's mother. We immediately liked the family and it seemed to us that they liked our house. While they were there, the young man said, *"If I write you an earnest money check tonight, will you take the sign down?"* and he made us a very reasonable offer. Mark and I looked at each other and we knew that our prayers had been answered. How cool was it that God had waited until the very end to send us a buyer! He had used that time for us to learn a little patience as well as to lean on Him to trust Him to work it all out in His timing. His timing was perfect after all – isn't it always? Because we had a buyer at the *end* of our construction process, we didn't have to move into an apartment temporarily. We did need to find a place for what we thought would be only three weeks – it turned into six weeks! We all stayed with my parents during this time and we made it work. But little did we know what an emotional roller coaster we were all in for!

We closed on our old house the first week in October. Pap-Paw's health had started to decline at this point and he had bypass surgery in late September. Immediately after his surgery, we noticed little things that he said as being *not quite right*. He stayed with my parents, along with the rest of us, during his recovery period which lasted several weeks. It wasn't the best of living conditions, but again we made it work – *not that it wasn't a bit trying at times for all of us!*

As we had begun to get closer to moving into our "new/old" home, Pap-Paw had told me that I could have many antiques from his home to place in our new home. My grandmother had quite a bit of furniture that she had inherited from her parents. My dad and I are both only children, so there was no one else in our family to whom to distribute the heirlooms. Grandma Dot had always promised me her Madame Alexander doll collection. She had a beautiful curio cabinet with lots of lovely dolls representing many different countries. She also had the Little Women collection and a few others. There was an old coat rack, a pie safe, and several others things. I was thrilled to get all these priceless pieces of furniture, yet a little sad because of the circumstances under which I would get them. However, God's timing is always best and I was very appreciative to have all this furniture to fill up our house. Grandma Dot was an avid family historian and kept all kinds of records on our family history. I believe she would be proud to know that the "historical" antiques from their families were now passed down to another generation that continues to enjoy them and take care of them.

While most of these possessions were promised *before* Pap-Paw's surgery, after he went back home to live by himself, he began this process of giving away everything. He gave many things to his sister, to my parents, and to Mark and me. His home was beginning to look a little bare; he had given away lamps, fine china, some small furniture, decorative pictures he removed from the walls, some guns, and he even gave my dad his truck. It seemed as if he was emptying out his whole house and keeping only what was necessary. There became a fine line between showing appreciation for what he was offering us versus not wanting to take everything the man had! He even wanted to give me his bed. He had two others, but I felt it was wrong to take the bed he slept in.

However, it was obvious that he was not pleased when he thought I didn't want it. It was also an antique and had belonged to my great-grandfather. He even told me, "*Your great-granddaddy died in that bed!*" I told him I would take it. He also tried to give me old junky items like severely used dishes – the kind that had been used for thirty-plus years that I might not even bother putting out at a yard sale. He was staying up all night and cleaning out drawers full of mementos, pictures, and all kinds of stuff. His personality changed and he began to turn on my dad, his only child and the one who had been his caregiver for the last several months. His thinking became illogical and irrational. He was easily agitated and angered. We all tried to handle him with kid gloves, but nothing seemed to make him happy.

Finally, on Election Day in November 2004, he seemed to have snapped. He called me on my cell phone and wanted me to come by his house, causing me to be late for work. He suddenly seemed to call everyone all the time and demand that we drop whatever we were doing and come directly to his aid, no matter how unimportant the matter. He had become angry with my dad over something very petty and unreasonable and refused to call him for anything. He was instead running Mark and me ragged with phone calls. During this time I had to work overtime on my job, live in my parents' house, move into a new home, and try to raise two small children!

On Election Day, Pap-Paw called me at work and told me that my dad had stolen $3,000.00 from him. I knew that couldn't be true, but he refused to listen to reason. My dad would not take anything from him, nor had my dad even been to his house during the last several days. This prompted a family feud of sorts. We knew my grandfather was not thinking right and that something must be medically wrong with him. He later found the money he had misplaced, but then illogically and wrongly accused my dad of sneaking back into his house during the night to replace the money he had taken. It was a nightmare! There was no convincing this man that my father was innocent of those ridiculous charges!

Our entire family was frazzled to pieces. Pap-Paw refused to go to the doctor. He had been released by his heart doctor and even though we suspected he had had a stroke, he absolutely would not consider going to the doctor or the hospital. His irrational behavior continued. He talked about changing his will. He suddenly began driving all around the city. He had basically stopped driving to town altogether a while back, and now he was racing around like Richard Petty.

One night while we were still staying with my parents, the phone rang about 4:00 in the morning. My mom answered it and Pap-Paw was on the other end asking for help and groaning. Mark, my dad and I jumped in the car and went over to his house. We found him lying on the kitchen floor with the telephone in his hand. The door was unlocked and Daddy and I immediately started telling him we loved him and trying to get him to wake up. Suddenly, when we mentioned calling 911, he was up and about! The paramedics came and he then suspiciously seemed fine. When they mentioned taking him to the ER to get checked out, he made the mistake of saying that he was going to get his gun. Then, the sheriff was called by EMS. I knew where Pap-Paw kept his pistol so I hid it from him. Of course, he later blamed my dad for taking that too!

EMS could not legally take Pap-Paw to the hospital that night because he refused. This nightmare we were living in went on for several more days. There was even more irrational behavior and it seemed the only option was to have him involuntarily committed. My dad and I even talked to one of our pastors one Sunday at church about what was going on. It was truly devastating. Pap-Paw attacked all of us verbally and said things that I hoped were not truly in his heart. That was what hurt the most – wondering if somewhere deep down inside, he really meant the things he said to us. We were also concerned about his living alone with this kind of behavior.

Eventually, my dad signed the paperwork to have him involuntarily committed. It was heartbreaking. I felt sick to my stomach. Why couldn't Pap-Paw have just gone to the hospital? I was literally unpacking boxes in my new home and my Pap-Paw was being picked up by sheriff's deputies and taken to who-knows-where. I remember just getting on my knees and praying that he would be okay. We were all in agreement as a family that it had to be done. It was just so incredibly sad.

He was taken to a mental hospital in Raleigh. They kept him there for almost a month. A doctor there evaluated him and it was determined that he had in fact had a stroke that affected the rational part of his brain and he was also diagnosed with dementia. She said that he would continue to get worse mentally so my dad made arrangements for him to live in a very nice assisted living facility back home. We spent Thanksgiving without him, while he was still in the hospital. It was one of the saddest Thanksgivings ever. Thankfully, by Christmas he was back in town and settled into his new place. Unfortunately, he was angry and unhappy. It was very hard to see him this way, but he eventually adjusted. My dad went to visit him *every* day. He would take him out to lunch and they would go for rides.

During all of this turmoil with Pap-Paw and our big move into our new home, I was required to work overtime on my job. We suddenly were ordered to work 12-hour days which was almost unheard of where we worked. We could take a short break for lunch and they would have it brought in to us. My family life and my new house suffered. It was a miserable time. I was very close to my grandparents and this situation with my grandfather took its toll on all of us. I began to think about the fact that Mark and I did not get pregnant when we tried a few months earlier. I could praise God that He didn't give me more than I could have handled at the time.

However, if any good was to come from all of the overtime work, it was the fact that we really needed the money. Just before Christmas, I was out shopping one night and Mark called me on my cell phone. He proceeded to tell me that we had somehow gone over budget on our house! I couldn't understand how that happened, because the entire time we were making decisions, we thought we were going to be *under* budget. We had even discussed the possibility of my being able to go part-time at work and be home with the kids after school! Now that wasn't going to happen. I again felt that familiar sick feeling in my stomach. I had just bought all these Christmas presents and I suddenly felt like we couldn't afford them.

Our money was tight. Mark was still getting acclimated to his sales job. He hadn't yet made a great deal in commissions and he didn't have a huge base salary. He had been counting on one big deal to come through at the end of the year, but it didn't happen. It turned out the company he was selling to didn't have any money either! I began to worry about our finances. I knew that God would provide our needs, but would that mean he would provide for them in another house? How embarrassing would it be to have to sell the house we just fixed up? We couldn't let Mark's family down. They had given us that land knowing that family would be living there! One Sunday in church, the pastor covered this passage of Scripture:

> **"Suppose one of you wants to build a tower. Will he not first sit down and estimate the cost to see if he has enough money to complete it? For if he lays the foundation and is not able to finish it, everyone who sees it will ridicule him, saying 'This fellow began to build and was not able to finish.'" Luke 14:28-30**

Ouch! I think our pride was a little wounded.

Our savings account was getting lower and lower. It seemed that each month we would have to transfer more money to pay our bills. We had just committed a few short months prior to sponsor a couple in Campus Crusade for Christ. They were at a large university in North Carolina and counting on us for their support. I began to question if we should have committed to give them any money at all. I am ashamed to admit that I even asked Mark if we should just tell them our situation and that we couldn't afford to help them anymore. Mark refused to do that. He strongly believes in tithing and he is a man of his word. We later found out that this couple had lost other sponsors and they, of course, were counting on us for financial support. I really appreciate my husband's faithfulness to tithe and to his word. God's Word says,

"'Will a man rob God? Yet you rob me.' But you ask, 'How do we rob you?' 'In tithes and offerings. You are under a curse – the whole nation of you – because you are robbing me. Bring the whole tithe into the storehouse that there may be food in my house. Test me in this,' says the Lord Almighty, 'and see if I will not throw open the floodgates of heaven and pour out so much blessing that you will not have room enough for it. I will prevent pests from devouring your crops, and the vines in your fields will not cast their fruit,' says the Lord Almighty. 'Then all the nations will call you blessed, for yours will be a delightful land,' says the Lord Almighty." Malachi 3:8-12

The Lord was most certainly faithful to us. Eventually, our finances began to take a turn for the better. We took out a home equity loan to consolidate the remaining house debt and car payments to a lower monthly payment and Mark began selling more software. We never regretted keeping our promise to our Campus Crusade couple and even now continue to sponsor them. We are thankful that God has used us to bless them as He has continued to bless us – so much that I sometimes feel like He has poured out so much blessing I can almost feel the floodgates of heaven opened up over us! To simply say that God is so good feels like an understatement.

Life Applications for Trusting God to Prove His Faithfulness

1. *Trust that God's timing is always perfect.* I am by nature a very impatient person. Sometimes the hardest thing is to sit back and wait for the Lord. However, that is what His Word precisely tells us to do.

   Key Scripture: **"I wait for the Lord, my souls waits, and in his word I put my hope." Psalm 130:5**

2. *Strength from past trials will serve to give us assurance that God will prove faithful in future trials.* Even though it is very hard to be joyful about going through trials, we can be certain that God will use these as opportunities to teach us something. We will later be able to use what we have learned when struggling in another trial. The more we see God's faithful work in our lives, the more faith we have that He will do it again!

   Key Scripture: **"Consider it pure joy, my brothers, whenever you face trials of many kinds, because you know that the testing of your faith develops perseverance." James 1:2-3**

3. *If we expect God to keep His promises to us, we must also keep our promises.* Tithing is not always a popular topic, but God instructs us to give Him one-tenth of the

first fruits of our income. Tithing is a way of being obedient to God and a way to show God that we trust Him. He knows our hearts, so therefore we should give with a cheerful, willing heart to further His kingdom. I am no way trying to say that God will make us rich as long as we tithe, but if we can show Him that we can be obedient in giving Him a tithe out of our small income, perhaps He will consider increasing our income, or at least providing little gifts back to us in other ways – tax refunds, department store sales, keeping our vehicles running like the Energizer bunny. God is good. If you're not already doing so, what bills or purchases could you possibly do without so that you might be able to tithe? Read the parable of the talents in Matthew 25: 14-28.

Key Scripture: "**His master replied, 'Well done, good and faithful servant! You have been faithful with a few things; I will put you in charge of many things. Come and share your master's happiness!'" Matthew 25:23**

Chapter Seven

Your Will, Not Mine

"'...Yet not as I will, but as you will.'"
Matthew 26:39

God had indeed been good to us and life was going pretty well. Mark and I had ultimately decided that we would not have any children together. My dreams of quitting my job and staying home with the kids seemed to be over. Although we were doing okay financially and we felt like we had at least dug ourselves out of a hole, I had simply come to the conclusion that I would be a working mother. After all, if we were going to be able to afford the things we were accustomed to – going out to eat, being able to buy the kids decent clothes, paying for their sports and other extracurricular activities, and taking a vacation every summer, it appeared that I would need to continue to work outside the home. It just seemed impossible that I would be able to stay home with the kids.

The summer of 2005 was a life-changing summer for us. I suddenly became surrounded with pregnant women. Mark's sister was pregnant with twin boys, my very good friend at work, Jenny, was pregnant with her second daughter, and another co-worker was also pregnant. Let me explain that when I said I was surrounded by pregnant women, I was in fact surrounded by them. You see, Jenny sat right beside me in the next cubicle, and the other pregnant co-worker sat on the other side of the cubicle from me. There was merely a partition separating us. It was in my face everywhere I turned! I was excited for them and helped plan baby showers for each of them. Just being around it, though, caused me to begin to question whether or not Mark and I would regret not having a baby together. One day at work, we were having a baby discussion and I said, *"If we are going to have any more children, I need to hurry up and decide."* Jenny said, *"You need to have your tubes tied!"* Although she didn't mean any harm in saying it, it really was a bit of a reality check for me. Did I really want my tubes tied? Was I ready to forever close the door to having a baby with Mark? That would be so final. It saddened me.

I nearly drove my poor husband crazy going back and forth on the matter! I felt so torn. Mark's sister gave birth to the twins in July just before we were to go on vacation. The night before we left for the beach, we drove to the hospital to see them. As I held one of them, I felt the tears well up in my eyes. It had been so long since I had held a tiny baby in my arms. Then, watching Mark's face light up as a proud uncle, I again felt the pangs of wonder. At Cherry Grove Beach, however, I enjoyed playing with Madison and Jackson in the ocean and feeling as free as a bird...or fish. I told myself that I didn't want to go back to diapers, bottles, and sleepless nights. My kids were at the perfect age to do fun things with and not have to be loaded down with everything but the kitchen sink whenever we wanted to take off and go anywhere.

I was happy just the way things were.

If I could have quit my job and stayed home with my kids, I might have felt differently. I just couldn't fathom the idea of continuing in my current job and trying to manage three kids with all of their extracurricular activities, staying out when they were sick, taking them to their doctor and dentist appointments...it just didn't make any sense. Mark's traveling schedule would make things difficult as well. My mother had always been there for Madison and Jackson, but she was getting older and I couldn't put the day-to-day responsibility of caring for a baby on her shoulders again. Mark's mother would be busy helping his sister with her twin babies, so there would certainly be competition in the babysitter department! I hated the idea of putting my child in daycare.

Madison and Jackson never had to go to daycare and from what I had heard it was so expensive that I may as well stay home if I had to pay out that much money for someone else to care for my baby! Again, our finances were okay, but my income was still needed to live comfortably. The health and dental insurance for our entire family was also through my employer, so that was also something to consider. Mark's plan was actually a little bit more expensive than mine. I felt trapped.

I was also protective of Madison and Jackson's feelings. After all, they had been through a lot with their parents' divorce at a very young age. I never wanted them to feel that Mark and I would love *our* child more than we love them. I also didn't want Mark or his family to unconsciously show favoritism to another child. Truthfully though, I knew Mark had enough love in his heart for all of them!

The Holy Spirit was not finished with me yet. Every time I thought about finalizing the baby decision and contemplating surgery, it gave me a sad, empty feeling. I remembered some time before, Mark had said to me, *"I just want somebody to call me Daddy."* That broke my heart. He had been so good to Madison and Jackson. Mark treated them as if they were his own. He even helped coach Jackson's tee-ball games; he was always there for both of them. The kids loved Mark and they referred to him as their dad when speaking to other people, but they called him "Mark." They called their biological father "Daddy." I never tried to force them to call Mark "Daddy." I felt it was unfair to expect them to do that while they still had a relationship with their dad. After all, it would hurt me to the bone if they referred to their stepmother as "Mama" – that was *my* name! Also, in one of our discussions about having a baby, Mark said, *"I can't imagine that we would ever look back and say that we wished we hadn't had this child."* How true that was! The bottom line was if it was God's will for us to have a baby, He would give us one! It soon became not a matter of preference in whether or not to have a baby, but a matter of obedience.

If I felt the nudging of the Holy Spirit (and I believe that I did), and yet did not act on what I felt He was calling me to do, whether it be out of fear, or convenience, or yes, even selfishness, then I would be disobedient. Also, I didn't want to live my life feeling guilty that I had deprived my husband of having his own child – his own flesh and blood. After wrestling with this issue for several weeks, I approached Mark again and we agreed that we would pray about it and we would try again to have a baby. We would give it six months and if nothing happened, we would assume it was not the Lord's will for us to have a baby. If He did allow us to become pregnant, we would just have to trust that He would provide a way for us to take care of the baby. I would either be able to quit my job, or God would provide some other form of reliable childcare. It was in His hands!

I had been listening to some CDs of a popular female Christian author and speaker that a friend had let me borrow. One particular CD really changed my life. She talked about going confidently before the throne and asking God for anything. In **1 John 5:14-15** it says, **"This is the confidence we have in approaching God: that if we ask anything according to his will, he hears us. And if we know that he hears us – whatever we ask – we know that we have what we asked of him."** What a powerful verse! However, the key words in this verse are *"his will"* – God's plan is always the best plan for our lives. We just need to be a team player. There is power in praying His will for our lives. In fact, Jesus himself models this in prayer twice in the Book of Matthew. First, in the Lord's Prayer:

> **"This, then, is how you should pray: "'Our Father in heaven, hallowed be your name, your kingdom come, *your will* be done on earth as it is in heaven. Give us today our daily bread. Forgive us our debts, as we also have forgiven our debtors. And lead us not into temptation, but deliver us from the evil one.'" Matthew 6:9-13 (Italics mine)**

Second, as He was praying in the Garden of Gethsemane, Scripture tells us, **"Going a little farther, he fell with his face to the ground and prayed, 'My Father, if it is possible, may this cup be taken from me. *Yet not as I will, but as you will.'"* Matthew 26:39 (Italics mine)** Jesus not only shows us how to surrender to God in heaven His will for our lives verbally, but also in His posture. He didn't just fall on His face to the ground because He was exhausted. It was an acknowledgement to the all-sovereign, all-powerful Father in heaven seated on His throne and an example of humility and reverence to us here on earth in how to approach our God in conveying our deepest needs to Him. Besides, God already knows what we need before we ask. (See Matthew 6:8) We do not need to fear the answer to our prayers according to His will because He is working all things for our good and to fulfill His purpose as Scripture tells us in Romans 8:28.

King David is known for being a man after God's own heart. He speaks of desiring to do God's will in **Psalm 40:8. "I desire to do *your will*, O my God; your law is within my heart."** (Italics mine) Again, in **Psalm 143:10**, David says, **"Teach me to do *your will*, for you are my God; may your good Spirit lead me on level ground."** (Italics mine) David was one of the few individuals mentioned in the Old Testament that God had filled with His Holy Spirit. David had learned through his life's failures the importance of obedience to God and allowing the Holy Spirit to guide him according to His will. A truly happy person allows himself to be submissive to the will of God in order to experience God's best for his life, praising God in all circumstances. David was a man who had realized this and was living this principle.

I distinctly remember kneeling beside my bed in prayer just pouring out my heart to God about our baby situation. The tears were flowing and I truly prayed a heartfelt prayer acknowledging if this was in fact His will I would accept that; and I would trust Him to handle all the details of childcare and whether or not I would be able to stay at home. It was the first time I trusted Him completely to handle it. It was a huge step of faith and yet I felt complete peace.

Not long after that, Mark and I went on a marriage retreat with our Bible Fellowship class to Lake Lure and stayed at the inn where the movie *Dirty Dancing* was filmed. It was a wonderful time and our class even had a prom night theme and we listened to old eighties music and danced. It was a blast! It was the perfect weekend to "start trying"! Again, this was in

God Keeps His Promises

God's hands and we were praying according to His will. Now this may seem a little far-fetched and weird to some, but I sincerely believe that at the exact moment of conception I was praying (in my head of course!), *"Your will, not mine...Your will, not mine..."*

The *very first* month we tried, we were pregnant! I will never forget the day I found out I was actually with child! I was experiencing some bodily changes and I suspected that it was a high possibility. Madison and Jackson were out of school that day for a teacher workday in October and we went to the Dixie Classic Fair. While sitting on the grass during the pig races (yes, I said *pig races* – we *do* live in the South, hence the *Dixie Classic Fair*), I felt extremely nauseous! The smoke from others around me in the crowd smoking cigarettes made it even worse. I couldn't wait to get out of there! Later, I was scheduled to have my hair cut. I was sitting in a chair at the salon waiting while a very pregnant lady was having her hair cut – she was the cousin of my friend and hairdresser, Cindy. The conversation was of course on babies, as she was getting ready to deliver any day!

Someone asked me if I thought we would have any more children and not being able to hold my thoughts inside any longer, I blurted out, *"I think I'm pregnant right now!!!"* I was encouraged by all the ladies to go straight to the pharmacy and buy a pregnancy test, so *I did.* I went back to my parent's house and Madison followed me into the bathroom. Within seconds we knew! Mark was out of town and I called him and gave him the news on the telephone because I couldn't wait for him to get home before I told him. He was having dinner by himself in Washington, DC. We were all so excited! Even Jackson, who I was most concerned about, said, *"Cool, I won't be the littlest anymore!"* We were joyful of this little life inside me and we knew God would provide a way to care for this child whether I worked or stayed home. He was saying to us loudly and clearly, that if we would trust Him, He would work out the details. Sometimes, God is just waiting for us to ask Him! And when we do, He **"is able to do immeasurably more than we could ask or imagine"**! Ephesians 3:20

Life Applications for Conforming to God's Will for Your Life

1. *Obey the nudging of the Holy Spirit.* From the time we accept Jesus as our Lord and Savior, the Holy Spirit comes to live in us. The closer we are to God, the easier it is to hear the Holy Spirit. Most of the time, I would suggest that we experience the guidance of the Spirit by little nudges. Perhaps He brings to mind a friend whom we haven't talked to in a while that may need us, or He may continue to give us ideas or thoughts about something that we believe are not our own thoughts. We may even resist those ideas if they are out of our comfort zone. If we believe God is speaking to us through His Holy Spirit, we should listen and obey these nudges.

    Key Scripture: "**However, as it is written: 'No eye has seen, no ear has heard, no mind has conceived what God has prepared for those who love Him' but God has revealed it to us by His Spirit.**" 1 Corinthians 2:9-10

2. *Pray His will for your situation.* Once you have felt the nudge of the Spirit, pray in order to determine if this is in fact His will. You can be sure that, if it is His will, it will happen!

    Key Scripture: "**This is the confidence we have in approaching God: that if we ask anything according** to his will, he hears us. And if we know that he hears us – whatever we ask – we know that we have what we asked of him." 1 John 5:14-15

3. *Obey His will for your situation.* This one is just what it says. We simply have to do whatever it is, although sometimes this may seem easier said than done if it is way out of our comfort zone. But we must obey!

   Key Scripture: **"Do not put out the Spirit's fire." 1 Thessalonians 5:19**

4. *Wait and watch Him work.* Again, if you are impatient like me, this can also be a tough thing to do. Sometimes we want to take control of the situation ourselves and get it done, or make it happen fast. We must align ourselves with God's timetable and be patient.

   Key Scripture: **"'Be still and know that I am God; I will be exalted among the nations, I will be exalted in the earth.'" Psalm 46:10**

Chapter Eight

Blessed Beyond Measure

> "Now to him who is able to do immeasurably more than all we ask or imagine, according to his power that is at work within us, to him be glory in the church and in Christ Jesus throughout all generations, for ever and ever! Amen."
> Ephesians 3:20-21

From the moment I knew I was expecting our baby, I can honestly say that I did not worry about childcare again. I somehow knew that God would bless our obedience to **"be fruitful and multiply" (Genesis 9:7)**. In return, Mark started selling some software! For the first time ever, he made his yearly sales quota at the end of 2005. It turned out to be an incredible year financially. While we were trying to be good stewards of that which He has blessed us with, we knew that He was affirming *"Yes, I will take care of this for you!"* In fact, I hesitate to say this at all for fear of sounding boastful, but do so only to let you know just how firm a "YES" we received from God and to give HIM ALL THE PRAISE AND GLORY! David speaks in **Psalm 34:1-4:**

> "I will extol the Lord at all times; his praise will always be on my lips. My soul will boast in the

Lord; let the afflicted hear and rejoice. Glorify the Lord with me; let us exalt his name together. I sought the Lord and he answered me; he delivered me from all my fears."

Again, David says in **Psalm 44:8** *"In God we make our boast all day long, and we will praise your name forever."* Early in 2006, not long before my due date, Mark made more money in a single month than I made in an *entire year!* Again, I'm only sharing this to prove how unbelievably good God is! That, and the fact that He must have a sense of humor because we certainly "got it." It was His plan for me to be a stay-at-home mom, and although it seemed impossible for us just a few short months before, nothing is impossible for God! Jesus himself tells us in **Matthew 19:26, "'With man this is impossible, but with God all things are possible.'" Jeremiah 32:27** even says, **"'I am the LORD, the God of all mankind. Is anything too hard for me?'"** I've often wondered since then if things might have turned out differently for us if we had not stepped out in faith and completely trusted God to work out those details. If we had expected less of God, actually not giving Him enough credit for what He was capable of doing, would I now be a stay-at-home mom? I believe God expects us to obey Him, ask Him specifically, and then to trust Him. He has been so good to us, and I believe He was just waiting for us to *ask Him!*

As a result of Mark's meeting his sales quota for 2005, we were given a rewards trip from his company. We could go anywhere we wanted to go, but the condition was that we must take the trip sometime in 2006. I remember the day that Mark called me and gave me the news. I was standing in my cubicle at work. All I could think of was either how pregnant I would be on a trip, or what would we do with an infant? It should have been an exciting, joyful moment, but instead of initially being happy about the trip, I whined and cried, *"Why now?...Can't they just give us the money instead? After all, I'm going to be quitting work; we need the money."*

I had always dreamed of going to Hawaii, and it didn't help matters that Mark and his first wife went there on their honeymoon. As I said earlier, we had both accumulated our marital debts from our divorces and, therefore, we ended up going to Charleston, SC for a few days instead of a long, romantic, paradise of a honeymoon. I had so often said to him, *"You **are** going to take me to Hawaii someday, right?"* Bless his heart, I'm sure he felt no pressure at all and I really shouldn't have placed those expectations on him, but it was truthfully a sore spot whenever anyone mentioned a trip to Hawaii because of what it reminded me of. To be completely honest, it made me jealous.

Well, now we finally had our chance to go, but we would either have to leave our kids and go when I was six months pregnant, or wait until after I had the baby and take two kids and an infant on that *long* flight, or leave all of them at home. It didn't seem fair or practical to do any of the above! After we discussed it and we had the blessing of my parents who would be keeping the children, we decided to go for it and go to Hawaii as a couple. We would have a second honeymoon before the baby came. Who knew how long it would be before we would have another chance to be alone and get any rest?

I immediately started planning the trip. Choosing Hawaii wasn't so simple. After all, there are several islands to choose from. Everyone hears a lot about Maui, but I had also heard that Kauai, "the garden island," was beautiful as well. Then, I also wanted to visit Pearl Harbor and see the USS Arizona

Memorial. We had to narrow this down and soon. We had decided to go in March and this was January!

My manager told me that Kauai was a beautiful place to go. He and his wife had been there and the way he described it made me want to go there. I had also seen a Travel Channel "Best Beaches for Kids" episode that showed the calm waters of Poipu Beach on Kauai. That's where I wanted to go! We purchased a *Fodor's Hawaii 2006* travel book and I went to work! I had almost planned everything I wanted to see and do when Mark called me one day at work and said that his boss said we might want to check into going to Maui. The owner of Mark's company had connections to a well-known luxury resort hotel and spa on Maui, and we were told that we could possibly get a good deal on our hotel. We had dreamed of going to Maui and actually staying at this place. It had also been featured on the Travel Channel and had an exclusive Spa Grande and an amazing waterslide with rapids, a Tarzan swing, and even a swim-up pool bar! As much as I hated to give up going to Kauai, it seemed like a chance of a lifetime to stay at this place and we may not always have those connections. Therefore, we changed our plans and booked a trip to Maui for seven nights, then our last night on Oahu where we stayed on Waikiki Beach and made a sight-seeing trip to Pearl Harbor.

All I can say is that God was in the planning of that trip! **Deuteronomy 31:8** tells us **"'The Lord himself goes before you and will be with you; he will never leave you nor forsake you. Do not be afraid; do not be discouraged.'"** That verse gives me great peace in planning trips. I truly believe that God's hand was upon us in choosing our destination. While we were in Maui, there were heavy rains on the islands around us. Guess which island was hardest hit? That's right…Kauai! In fact, I still have a newspaper from our trip that week as a

God Keeps His Promises

souvenir. The front page of The Maui News says "Kauai dam bursts – one dead, as many as seven others missing after 2 houses swept away."3 It was horrendous. We later met a couple at the airport in Honolulu as we were waiting to board the plane on our way home. They had been on a Hawaiian cruise and were so disappointed. The lady told me that when they docked in Kauai there were terrible rains, flooding, and mudslides. The captain had to call everyone back to the ship to depart. My heart went out to them. We had been so fortunate because at our location on Maui we only had some overcast days. Once, during an evening luau, it began to shower and we were all given ponchos to wear during the performance, but it certainly wasn't bad. We felt so blessed and thankful that our mighty God, who is so good to us, made sure that we ended up in just the right spot. How miserable and heartbroken I would have been if we had flown all that way only to have to sit in a hotel room the entire time and not be able to do any sightseeing or enjoy any of the beaches because of the weather.

In fact, we had a marvelous trip! We dined at some of the most delicious, exotic restaurants, where we enjoyed the most breathtaking views I've ever seen while tasting some of the most mouthwatering cuisine I've ever eaten! On Maui, we went to the top of Mount Haleakala, a volcano crater, to see the sunrise. It *would* have been beautiful if the clouds hadn't blocked the sunrise. It was absolutely freezing at 10,000 feet above sea level, but it was something I'll never forget. We went on an evening dinner cruise, to the Old Lahaina Luau, and on a whale watching cruise – my personal favorite! We even made the long, curvy, edge of the cliff drive to Hana where we saw some fabulous waterfalls along the way. I even somehow managed *not* to get carsick! On Oahu, we did see the USS Arizona Memorial which was certainly worth the trip. It was truly the trip of a lifetime and the precious bambino in my belly was quite the little trooper!

When we returned home, things began to get back to normal. I continued to work as I got bigger and bigger. I couldn't wait for this baby to come. When we had our sonogram, the doctor was unable to inform us if the baby was a boy or a girl. Mark's sister used to work as a nurse for an OB/GYN so she took our videotape to a friend in her office that read sonograms. Within about a minute, she was able to say it was a boy! We had scheduled a 3-D sonogram with my doctor's office for late March. It was awesome the way they could take pictures of the baby inside of me and the photographs actually looked like a baby and not a blob! We could actually see our son's face. It was incredible.

I had a wonderfully healthy, happy pregnancy, but as we approached the due date I was growing impatient. I couldn't wait to have this baby and begin my life as a stay-at-home mother. I just knew this baby would come before his due date. After all, this was my third child. I couldn't believe it when I went past my due date. Finally, my doctor agreed to induce me on Father's Day, the 18th of June. I kept hoping that the little one would decide to come out before then because I was so miserable. Early that Sunday morning, I began having contractions. I said to Mark, *"Well, I'm scheduled to be induced today anyway. We might as well go on over and see if anything's happening."* I took time to send out an email for anyone in our Bible Fellowship class that was possibly up and on the computer before they headed to church, requesting prayer for a smooth and speedy delivery with no complications.

Once we arrived at the hospital and got checked in, those labor pains started increasing. By lunchtime, he was ready to come out. Our mothers had gone downstairs to the cafeteria to grab some lunch and they had to be called back up in a hurry! Bryson Olin Long made his grand entrance after only about three pushes at 1:33 pm. Both of his grandmothers were there when he made his debut. Mark's mother even cut the cord! Prayers were again answered because I had never had such an easy delivery.

I remember thinking what a glorious Father's Day! It seemed fitting for a man who had loved my children as his own for so long to finally experience the birth of his own flesh and blood on the day set aside to honor fathers. Madison and Jackson were with us as well and I was so glad it worked out that way so we could all be together as a family in the labor and delivery room.

It was a precious day – one we will never forget. Did I mention that Bryson looks just like his daddy?

Christy Long

Life Applications for Receiving God's Blessings

1. *Nothing is too hard for God, but sometimes He is just waiting for us to ask.* It would be silly for us to think that there is something, no matter how large or small, that God could *not* do in our lives. He created the universe, He is responsible for every living breathing creature, and He turns the world on its axis. How ridiculous then to think that any of our problems or needs would be too great for Him, no matter how huge and significant they seem to us. He wants to give us what we ask according to His will – *but He does want us to ask!*

   Key Scripture: **"Jesus looked at them and said, 'With man this is impossible, but with God all things are possible.'" Matthew 19:26**

2. *He is able to bless us beyond our wildest dreams!*

   Key Scripture: **"Now to him who is able to do immeasurably more than all we ask or imagine, according to his power that is at work within us…" Ephesians 3:20**

3. *We can trust God to take care of the details.* God will do what He promises. We just need to pray and believe Him to do it.

Key Scripture: **"Do not be anxious about anything, but in everything, by prayer and petition, with thanksgiving, present your requests to God." Philippians 4:6**

4. *Get to know Him as your Abba, Father.* If we have a personal relationship with Jesus Christ, we are God's children. He loves us as a father loves his children. No matter how good, bad, or mediocre your own father is/was, we have a heavenly Daddy that wants to pour out blessings on us. Let Him know how much you love Him!

Key Scripture: "**Because you are sons, God sent the Spirit of his Son into our hearts, the Spirit who calls out, 'Abba, Father.' So you are no longer a slave, but a son; and since you are a son, God has made you also an heir." Galatians 4:6-7**

Chapter Nine

Desires of My Heart

"Delight yourself in the Lord and He will give you the desires of your heart." Psalm 37:4

After Bryson was born, I thankfully became a stay-at-home mom. Finally, my dream of being home with my children had come true! Some days I just wanted to pinch myself. I would drop Madison and Jackson off at school in the mornings and almost would inadvertently take a left turn out of the school parking lot and head to the credit union! It seemed like I was playing hooky by hanging a right and going back home. Life had changed and although it seemed like the day would never get here while I was working, I was now living my dream and it almost seemed "too good to be true."

I had three precious children and a wonderful, godly husband. I was living in my dream house. Although nothing spectacular for most people, our home of course had special meaning for us. I had always loved white farm houses and it was just what I wanted. We had a little piece of land surrounded by acres and acres of family land around us – a little piece of heaven out in the country. Inside our home, we had family treasures from both our families – an old hutch that Mark's great-great-grandfather built, a wooden chest that he had built and given to his grandson (Mark's grandpa) for high school graduation with a carved inscription on the wood indicating that it was a "present" for graduation. There are also many heirlooms from my family line: an admired hat tree stands in the foyer, a couple of tables in the living room, some antique lamps, a pie safe, a dry sink, a water bowl and pitcher, my grandmother's doll she had from the time she was two years old. My Pap-Paw had even given me the old antique organ that his mother played at their church when he was growing up. These items may not mean much to most people, but they represent something special to us.

We love our home because of the memories that were once made here and the memories that are yet to be made! We held open house about a year after we moved and became settled in for our friends and family since we had fixed up the home place. On the front of the invitation, we had copied a picture of the house as it looked before the renovations with the verse, **"For the Lord is good and his love endures forever; his faithfulness continues through all generations." Psalm 100:5** God has indeed proven Himself to be so faithful. Often, the verse, **"Delight yourself in the Lord and He will give you the desires of your heart," Psalm 37:4** comes to mind. I am so thankful to God for what He has given us and allowed us to enjoy for a time. I truly do feel that I have been given the *"desires of my heart."*

However, these precious antiques also serve in my home as a reminder to me that we can't take it with us when we go! These were someone else's possessions, someone who lived before us, and while I'm sure they enjoyed them, they are earthly things – material things. Sometimes I just feel as though I could burst with thankfulness for what God has blessed us with for a time, but please let me be clear with the message I'm trying to convey. I used to place a lot of importance on house, cars, clothes, and money in general. Over the last several years, the Lord has shown me that if those are the things we are focusing our desires on, then we've got it all wrong. It has become clear to me that for the short time we are here on earth our priority should be God and then relationships. All the other things will pass away or be passed on to someone else.

My Pap-Paw went to be with the Lord on December 8, 2006. My dad and I were both with him when he went to his heavenly home. I miss him so much and look forward to seeing him again. I am also very grateful to God that He allowed me to be home during his illness. I was able to visit him in the hospital and in the assisted living facility more during those last few months since I was no longer employed. We celebrated his 90th birthday with a party at our home in June of that year. God's timing is always perfect.

When I think of my grandfather's life, I remember this verse: **"A good man leaves an inheritance for his children's children." Proverbs 13:22a** My grandparents have given me a new appreciation for living moderately. As my dad spent many long hours cleaning out my grandparents' house, and I spent a *few short* hours, we realized that our "stuff" that's so important to us may not be worth anything to someone else. It's all meaningless in the end. Solomon writes in **Ecclesiastes 2:18, "I hated all the things I had toiled for under the sun, because I must leave them to the one who comes after me."** My point is this: as women, it is in our design to want to stay in the latest fashion and have our houses decorated with the latest trends, but eventually (in fact, very soon) those new styles will be *out of style* and what's left in our closets and drawers will just end up going to Goodwill or some other charitable organization that probably doesn't want them either!

Now please don't misunderstand, I still like shoes and purses like any other normal female, but it has caused me to stop and ponder over my purchases in a way that I never did before. Jesus himself said,

> **"'Do not store up for yourself treasures on earth, where moth and rust destroy, and where thieves break in and steal. But store up for yourselves treasures in heaven, where moth and rust do not destroy, and where thieves do not break in and steal. For where your treasure is, there your heart will be also.'" Matthew 6:19-21**

If we are children of God, we are on a pilgrimage here on earth. This is not going to be our eternal home; we are just passing through. As Christians, we must focus on the spectacular beauty that awaits us in our heavenly home. No mansion on earth could compare with what lies beyond in glory. Again, Jesus said,

> **"In my Father's house are many rooms. If it were not so, I would have told you. I am going there to prepare a place for you." John 14:2**

Can you even imagine what kind of place Jesus has prepared for you? I can't, but it's got to be better than anything we've experienced here.

The years 2006 and 2007 were also great for software sales. Through Mark's company, we received another rewards trip. This time we decided to take the kids and Mark's mother (as Nana/Nanny) to Maui. I had promised Madison the previous year that if we were able to go again, we would make it a family trip. It was an awesome family vacation. I remember just feeling so blessed to be going back with the kids. They enjoyed it so much and we made so many wonderful memories – a snorkeling cruise, the spa (all the girls went together), and the pool at the resort had all kinds of kid-friendly waterslides. As I write this book, we are planning another family trip this August. Again, sometimes I feel the need to pinch myself. We are so undeserving of these trips – in no disrespect to my dear husband who has worked very hard to earn them from his company, and we as a family must make sacrifices during the course of the year due to his travels. Ultimately though, all things come from God above and He has the power to give and take away. He has been so good to us in all areas. I never want to get to the point of feeling too comfortable with things of the world.

As I write this portion of the book, our nation's economy seems to be taking a downturn. Gas prices have been at a record high with no predictions of significantly coming back down in the near future, the stock market is unstable, and Mark just had the worst sales quarter he has had since 2005. I am constantly reminded where our daily bread comes from. I recently read a Proverbs 31 devotion that instructed we are not to rely on "yesterday's bread." I do not know what His plans are for the rest of my life, but I do know as I learned some time ago that it is to give me **"hope and a future" (Jeremiah 29:11).** Life is hard sometimes and the road we walk as Christians is not easy. The only real thing we can depend on is Jesus. He will be there to walk with us no matter what kind of trial we are going through. Just as the Lord said to Joshua, **"'As I was with Moses, so I will be with you; I will never leave you nor forsake you.'" (Joshua 1:5b)** That remains true even today.

As I continue on my Christian walk, the "desires of my heart" are veering away from things like a big house, a new vehicle, luxurious reward trips (although I'm still looking forward to August!), and more toward things like becoming a woman after God's own heart. I am incredibly thankful that I have been able to stay home with my children for almost two years now. I have become involved in Women of the Word (WOW) Bible study at our church on Wednesday mornings. I have been available to be the grademother for my son's class and to be more active in my children's school activities. There are so many things that I have been privileged to take part in since I am no longer working outside the home. I pray that God would have me continue in my role as a stay-at-home mom at least until my youngest starts kindergarten.

My true desires are spending time with my family, taking part in Bible studies, focusing on my relationship with Jesus, and gaining a deeper knowledge of the Bible. It is my heart's desire to leave a legacy for my children. I want them and future generations, if the Lord tarries, to know what it means to have a relationship with Jesus. I have already told my oldest two that that is the single most important decision they will ever make in their lifetime! It was said by a wise older lady in one of my small group Bible studies that *God gives us the desires we have*. I believe with all my heart that He has given me the desire to write this book, an account of my life and God's faithfulness to my family and me. If He chooses to see that it is published and it actually reaches more people than just my friends and family, well then, that's just a bonus! I have felt a real urgency, especially within the last month or so to finish the task I feel He has called me to do. In fact, I have kept the verse, **"I will hurry, without lingering, to obey your commands," Psalm 119:60 NLT** on my keyboard.

Easter was just a few weeks ago and it has been a tradition in my family to put flowers on the graves of our loved ones that have gone before us. I used to accompany my grandparents to God's Acre in the Moravian cemetery to scrub the flat white marble stones with Comet cleaner, a brush and water, and then place flowers on the graves. In the Moravian graveyard the stones are all flat because it signifies equality in God's eyes. Almost all of them have a Bible verse or a saying of some kind to represent the person's life. Although I will not be buried there because I am no longer Moravian, I have often thought about what verse I would want to be engraved on my stone. This year, my dad found the gravesites of my great-great-grandparents in a nearby cemetery and placed flowers on them. What we found on my great-great-grandmother's stone was a powerful statement that pretty much sums it all up. It said, *"I am resting in my Savior's arms and it's all right."* Wow! I can't wait to meet her in heaven! That certainly gives me great comfort in knowing where she is.

As Moses preached to the Israelites as they were about to go into the Promised Land, **"Only be careful, and watch yourselves closely so that you do not forget the things your eyes have seen or let them slip from your heart as long as you live. Teach them to your children and to their children after them." Deuteronomy 4:9** Perhaps this is one of the main reasons for writing down all the ways the Lord has worked in my life and how He has blessed us. As Christians, we all have a story or hopefully many stories we can share with our children and others of what our mighty God has done for us. He alone is worthy of our praise. Let's give Him all the glory! What better way to equip our children in life than by our own testimony, that they might know the Word of God is alive and it is the Truth.

Another desire of my heart is to perhaps minister to women who are going through or have been through a difficult time as a result of a broken marriage or some other circumstance. I continue to hear of more and more ladies that have found themselves in places they never thought they would be. No marriage is beyond the attack of the enemy. While couples can certainly take precautions to guard their marriages through prayer and setting appropriate boundaries as a hedge of protection, Satan is there lurking, waiting to pounce as soon as he has an opportune time. Marriages that so many of us on the outside thought were nearly perfect have crumbled.

There are so many hurting women (and men) as result of failed marriages. First, the message I want to deliver is this:

"Praise be to the God and Father of our Lord Jesus Christ, the Father of compassion and the God of all comfort, who comforts us in all our troubles, so that we can comfort those in any trouble with the comfort we ourselves have received from God." 2 Corinthians 1:3-4

In fact, as I have been completing this chapter of the book, I registered a domain name with Google with hopes of eventually being able to promote this book. Within just two days, the Lord placed an urgent burden on my heart to create a website with my testimony and encouragement to other women that may be going through a difficult circumstance. Comfort to Comfort Ministries, based on the above scripture, was born. I'm not sure what God would have me do just yet, but if I can encourage just one person, then it will have served its purpose. There is something about knowing someone who has been where you are, someone who has faced a trial similar to yours and not only survived, but *thrived*; about seeing how God worked things out for her good because He had a better plan and a higher purpose for her life. **James 1:2-3** tells us to **"consider it pure joy, my brothers, whenever you face trials of many kinds, because you know that the testing of your faith develops perseverance."** Let's face it though, how many of us really consider it pure joy when we are going through a trial? Certainly, it's a tough thing to do, but I believe it helps to know of someone else that has been there and through the grace and love of Jesus Christ his or her life is better than before. That is a message that brings hope and is what I pray that I can accomplish through these pages.

Second, **Romans 8:18** promises that we are not suffering in vain. **"I consider that our present sufferings are not worth comparing with the glory that will be revealed in us."** God would only allow us to suffer if it were to be used for His glory – His purpose – His bigger plan in the grand picture as it relates to eternity. Sometimes we may never know this side of heaven what His reasons are, but we must trust Him, that He will use our story for His good. Ultimately, the *desire of my heart* is to be used by God, to somehow serve a role as only He sees fit, in furthering the kingdom for His glory.

Life Applications for Finding True Happiness

1. *Delight yourself in the Lord.* Spend time with Jesus both in the fellowship of prayer and reading His Word. Perhaps take part in a Bible study. Ask Him to fill you with His Holy Spirit so that you are thirsty for more.

   Key Scripture: **"Delight yourself in the Lord and he will give you the desires of your heart." Psalm 37:4**

2. *Allow Him to transform your desires to meet His desires for you.* As we do more of the above, our hearts will eventually change to become more like His, as well as our desires.

   Key Scripture: **"Search me, O God, and know my heart; test me and know my anxious thoughts. See if there is any offensive way in me, and lead me in the way everlasting." Psalm 139:23-24**

3. *It's all about Jesus!* Stay focused on what is most important right now on this earth. View this life as a pilgrimage to heaven. That puts it all in perspective!

   Key Scripture: **"Brothers, I do not consider myself yet to have taken hold of it. But one thing I do: Forgetting what is behind and straining toward what is ahead, I press on toward the goal to win the prize** for which God has called me heavenward in Christ Jesus." Philippians 3:13-14

4. *Pass it on!* When God gets you through your trial, use what He has taught you to help others. Do not let your suffering be in vain! Let the God of all comfort who has comforted you, show you how to comfort others.

Key Scripture: **"Praise be to the God and Father of our Lord Jesus Christ, the Father of compassion and the God of all comfort, who comforts us in all our troubles, so that we can comfort those in any trouble with the comfort we ourselves have received from God." 2 Corinthians 1:3-4**

God Keeps His Promises

Chapter Ten

Healer of My Heart

"He heals the brokenhearted and binds up their wounds." Psalm 147:3

This verse has become very dear to me over the last several months, and yet this chapter is perhaps the hardest for me to write. It is difficult, not because it causes me pain, but rather attempting to accurately explain just how and when this healing took place. The healing process was exactly that – *a process!* In fact, those who knew me at the time of my separation and two, three, maybe even four years after my divorce remember the sarcasm and bitterness that I am sure was evident in my everyday conversations when the subject turned to my ex-husband.

Without going into detail about everything that happened between us and all the hurtful emotions that I carried, at the very least I felt betrayed. I had a daughter who was a toddler while expecting another baby, then giving birth to a son, and all the while helplessly watching the hardening of my husband's heart through that process, and then, to finally see him make the choice to walk away. It was a horribly painful experience; one that almost seemed surreal. Yet, if I could go back and replay some things that happened in my life during that time, I certainly would have handled things much differently, or at least I hope so. Maybe if I had been further along in my walk as a Christian I would have exhibited more Christ-like behavior, but I know there were many strong Christian brothers and sisters that fervently prayed *for* me and I will be forever grateful for their intercession on my behalf. God can change hearts and He has changed mine. The power of the Holy Spirit has done a work on the inside of me, and Jesus deserves all the praise and glory! Having said these things, I believe there are three important components that have significantly contributed to my healing process – seeking godly counsel, learning to apply God's Word to my personal situation, and time.

First, seeking godly counsel is essential. If we listen to what the world has to say about divorce or any other problem we encounter, I'm afraid we are going to be severely misled. I would recommend a good *Christian* counselor to anyone going through a separation or other difficult circumstance. My husband and I did see a wonderful Christian counselor, but that should not be any reflection on the outcome of our situation. I am convinced that a good Christian counselor will advise an individual or a couple to the best of his or her ability based on what is *biblically true* and not necessarily what is generally accepted by the world. I know for me personally, if I am having a problem, I want to know what God's Word has to say about the situation that I am in and how He would expect me to handle it.

Also, most of us need to talk through our situation with another person – it is truly therapeutic to the soul to get things off your chest. Our friends and family members may not always be the best qualified to give us the advice we need to hear, and we may eventually drive them crazy if we talk to them *too much* about our problems (I know I have certainly been guilty of this!). Therefore, if we are constantly finding ourselves in a "need to talk" state, why not talk to someone who is qualified to help us process our emotions? I might also add that we can always talk to Jesus. His line is never busy and He stays up all night. There is no greater counselor than the One and Only God Almighty who we can have a personal relationship with, and He doesn't charge by the hour!

As I mentioned previously, we are privileged to have Dr. Gary Chapman on the staff of my church as our Senior Associate Pastor. He is well-known throughout the world and has written many books on marriage and other relational topics; probably his best known book is *The Five Love Languages*. Since I joined in 2000, I have been blessed to hear Dr. Chapman speak through his sermons and other events. I am sure it is no accident that I have heard him speak on the topic of *anger* several times. Previously, I had become familiar with the passage in Romans when Paul warns us not to take revenge, but rather be kind to your enemies.

> **"Do not take revenge, my friends, but leave room for God's wrath, for it is written: 'It is mine to avenge; I will repay,' says the Lord. On the contrary: 'If your enemy is hungry, feed him; if he is thirsty, give him something to drink. In doing this, you will heap burning coals on his head.' Do not be overcome by evil, but overcome evil with good." Romans 12:19-21**

Like a lot of other people, I had always interpreted this verse to mean that if I were kind to my enemies, or *"killed them with kindness,"* that it would be just like I was heaping burning coals on their heads; and, truthfully, the thought of burning coals on their heads appealed to me! Dr. Chapman explained that this is not at all what this verse means. In fact, it means just the opposite. He explained that in biblical times, people carried burning coals used to heat their homes in baskets on top of their heads. Therefore, this verse actually means not only to feed your enemies, and give them something to drink, but also to help them stay warm!

In his book *The Five Love Languages of Apology*, Dr. Chapman devotes an entire chapter to *forgiveness*. When asked how many times we should forgive, Jesus tells us, **"seventy-seven times."** (See Matthew 18:22) Of course this is not meant to be an actual number of forgiveness passes we extend until they expire, but we should *always* be willing to forgive if there is true repentance. Jesus also said, **"For if you forgive men when they sin against you, your heavenly Father will also forgive you. But if you do not forgive men their sins, your Father will not forgive your sins."** Matthew 6:14-15 I don't know about you, but I want to be forgiven for my sins. I know I have most definitely not lived a perfect life free from sin, and I need my heavenly Father to forgive me. If He can forgive me, can I not forgive someone else?

Next, in a case in which someone has wronged us, it is often so easy to judge the offender. I know in my own situation, this was something I dealt with for quite a while. I wanted the most severe punishment to be handed down to the one that I felt had betrayed and hurt me. Again, we should apply what Jesus said, **"Do not judge, or you too will be judged. For in the same way you judge others, you will be judged, and with the measure you use, it will be measured to you."** Matthew 7:1-2 Okay, again, I know I have messed up plenty of times in my life. Somehow we tend to look at the sin of others and feel that it is far worse than our own, but sin is sin in the eyes of God. This passage of Scripture is very humbling for me and has actually played an important part in my getting over some of my hurts and wounds.

Maybe someone has done something horrible to you and you feel he or she should be punished severely. Now, think about the worst thing you've ever done, something maybe no one but God knows about. Do we want God to judge us with the same severity we wanted Him to judge the other person? Somehow when I think of it that way, I can find the capability to find mercy inside of me. We are all human beings here on planet earth and we live in a fallen world. Until Jesus comes, we will unfortunately continue to make mistakes and so will our loved ones. Let's show each other grace and mercy so our heavenly Father will in turn choose to show it to us, because we can be sure that we will need it!

What if the person who wronged or betrayed you never had a repentant heart and never asked for your forgiveness? Funny you should ask! This was the case in my own situation, and Dr. Chapman has covered this scenario as well. This may be the single most important factor that has contributed to my complete and total healing. As I said earlier, I was very angry and bitter for a time over what had happened in my life. It was a terrible thing to get over and I was resentful and hurt. No one ever asked for my forgiveness. Does that mean I don't have to forgive? Yes, I don't *have* to forgive, but forgiving someone isn't just for the other person. If we continue to carry around the anger and hurt it will make us bitter. It's hard to love others when we are bitter.

In *The Five Love Languages of Apology*, Dr. Chapman writes, "So the person who is feeling hurt and angry toward another who has treated him unfairly is to release that person to an all-knowing heavenly Father who is fully capable of doing what is just and right toward that person. Jesus gave us the model. The apostle Peter said of Jesus, "'**When they hurled their insults at him, he did not retaliate; when he suffered, he made no threats, Instead, he entrusted himself to him who judges justly.**'" (1 Peter 2:23 NIV) As a man, Jesus did not take revenge on those who had wronged Him; rather, He committed the whole situation to God, knowing that God would judge righteously."4 Does that automatically make the hurt go away? Absolutely not! But the first step is recognizing that the situation is out of my control and letting God handle it. There is tremendous freedom in giving it over to God rather than holding onto it. Do we want to be bitter or *better*? Again, one of my favorite verses is **Romans 8:28,**

> **"And we know that in all things God works for the good of those who love him, who have been called according to His purpose."**

No matter what our circumstance, God can use it for His good and for our good, but we have to be willing to turn it over to *Him.* To quote Jesus again,

> **"You have heard that it was said, 'Love your neighbor and hate you enemy.' But I tell you: Love your enemies and pray for those who persecute you, that you may be sons of your Father in heaven. He causes his sun to rise on the evil and the good, and sends rain on the righteous and the unrighteous. If you love those who love you, what reward will you get? Are not even the tax collectors doing that? And if you greet only your brothers, what are you doing more than others? Do not even pagans do that? Be**

perfect, therefore, as your heavenly Father is perfect." Matthew 5:43-48

Quite frankly, if we love only those who love us, we are no different from anyone else and we are not living as children of God. We cannot be effective Christians if we harbor any hate in our hearts, nor can we ever be truly happy and blessed.

I realize I have referenced quite a bit of Scripture in this chapter, but it is absolutely instrumental in the healing process. Reading and applying God's Word is like medicine for a wounded soul. There is nothing we will face in life that isn't covered in the Instruction Book – the Bible!

Finally, we've all heard the old adage, "Time heals all wounds." Well, I would like to correct it just a bit – *"Time and Jesus heal all wounds."* While time alone may well help, without the grace and healing of Jesus Christ, it may also cause the bitterness to fester. In my case, the healing did not take place immediately. It was certainly a gradual process – I found that the closer my relationship with Jesus became, and the more I tried to apply God's Word to my daily life, the more my heart healed. This past year, while doing my homework for the Beth Moore study, *A Woman's Heart: God's Dwelling Place*, Beth said, "You will never maximize your gifts and God-given talents until you have camped by the healing springs. Why wait any longer? We are here for such a brief time. In order to heal, you may need to start by forgiving. Yet you may fear as I did, 'If I forgive, that will make it all right, and it's not all right.' Let God whisper into your ear what He whispered to me: 'No, My Child; forgiving will make you all right.'"[5] On that same page, one of the passages of Scripture we were to look up was **Psalm 147:3, "He heals the brokenhearted and binds up their wounds."** How very true! At the time, I was on a ladies' beach trip with a wonderful group of ladies from my Bible Fellowship class and I was actually doing my homework out on the deck by the ocean in the morning while having my coffee. I immediately grabbed two index cards and wrote that verse on them; one for myself, and another for a dear lady I had gotten to know that weekend who was separated from her husband. It has become a favorite verse that I have prayed for her and for others that I know are hurting. It struck me that morning that the Lord had not only healed my broken heart, but He had in fact bound up the wounds. I no longer felt any of the pain from that terrible nightmare. Of course I still have memories, but the sting is no longer there.

My personal story of healing has provided opportunities to reach out to my ex-husband's family over the last year or so. Early on, I know I said and did things out of my anger and hurt that I wish I could change, but overall I have always tried to keep my children's best interest in mind. I have determined that I alone am responsible for my own actions. I will have to answer to God for the things *I* have done regardless of what was done *to me*. I remember when I was newly separated and was obviously angry toward my ex-husband, someone who was a product of a broken home herself, passed on some advice to me. She said the best thing my ex-husband and I could do would be to try and remain friends for the children's sake. At the time I thought she was out of her mind! However, as time has gone by I realize the wisdom in her statement. My children should not have to suffer any more than they already have for being in the situation they are in. The very least we can do is respect one another and treat each other cordially, respectfully, and basically the way the other would like to be treated. Only by the grace of God could this be possible, but what I'm telling you is true. God is perfectly capable of healing hearts and repairing damaged relationships.

In August of this past year, my former father-in-law was honored at a high school football game where he had coached at one time. The high school football field was named after him and his family was given special treatment and seating at the game, and they all went out on the field at half time for the presentation. Because I had my children on that Friday night (their dad was coaching the opposing football team at the game), my husband and I were invited to sit with my ex-husband's family and friends at the game. It was almost a reunion of sorts as I saw my former sister-in-law who lives out-of-state and her kids, who had really grown up. Everyone was so nice to each other, even my ex-husband's wife's family talked to us and we were actually friendly to each other. It wasn't even a fake sort of friendly; it was genuine. It was also a bittersweet evening because my former father-in-law had recently been diagnosed with pancreatic cancer. My husband even commented the next day that it was weird because *everybody was so nice to each other!* It was almost unbelievable. I was just so thankful that we had come that far.

During the next several months, my former father-in-law became very ill. My children and I prayed for him every day and I grew more concerned as he was hospitalized for about two or three weeks prior to Christmas. Early morning on the day after Christmas, the phone woke me up. It was my ex-husband telling me with a quiver in his voice that his daddy wasn't doing well. He said that it was probably just a matter of time and that I should probably go ahead and prepare the kids. I told him I would be praying for his dad and that I would pray for him too. My heart was so heavy that day as I visualized the family congregating at the hospital. We talked again later that evening and he gave me an update. Just before midnight, I awoke to a ringing telephone again. He told me that his daddy had died just a short while before. The next morning as I broke the news to my children, I asked them if they would like for me to take them to visit their daddy and Maw-Maw. Then, I suggested that we even take them some food. I called first to make sure he didn't mind if we visited for a little while and brought some food. He graciously accepted and I started cooking.

Visiting with the family was emotional for me. His mother was crying and we said kind and comforting words to each other. My former sisters-in-law were there and we talked and they showed me pictures they were going through to display at the funeral home. For a brief while, it felt as though I were still a part of the family. I remember thinking that day that it is no wonder God's plan is for one man and one woman for life. I certainly am not wishing at this point that I were still with my ex-husband, but when two people marry, and especially when they have children together, there will always be a connection to family. Divorce is never God's plan. I truly loved my ex-husband's family. There were nieces and nephews that I knew from the time they were toddlers and some before birth. My sister-in-law and I were pregnant at the same time with our daughters and I went on several family vacations with all of them. While the divorce has created a distance between us, I still deeply care for his family.

Perhaps the strongest evidence to me that so much healing has taken place was when my ex-husband gave me a long, heartfelt hug as I was leaving that day and thanked me for everything. I could hardly believe it then, and he even hugged me a second time in the line at the funeral home. He said to me, *"You know Daddy always thought a lot of you."* Those words brought tears to my eyes. Then, I even hugged his wife.

God Keeps His Promises

After the visitation at the funeral home, Madison invited her cousin to spend the night with us and go to church with us the next day. I am thankful that we experience the freedom to allow our children to be close. There is no barrier between us because of the divorce; Madison's cousins are not restricted from coming to her house because I am the *ex-wife*, and for that I am thankful.

This past summer he took the kids to Disney World, so they were actually gone an extra week as they also went on their annual beach trip with his family. As much as I missed them, I am thankful their dad is a part of their lives. The dates of their Disney trip included Madison's birthday. At first, it made me a little sad, but I have come to realize that it's not about me. What a cool way to spend your birthday!

The relationship we have now is probably as good as it can be. It is only through the power of God and His grace that we have come this far. There was so much hurt just a few short years ago and it now seems like it was another lifetime ago. There are so many ways the Lord has worked on me and I thank Him that He is not finished with me yet! I pray that this will provide a source of comfort and possibly even give hope for those who are still hurting and in need of some healing. God deserves ALL the GLORY and that is why this was written FOR HIS GLORY. Always remember that GOD KEEPS HIS PROMISES!

God Keeps His Promises

Life Applications for Healing

1. *Open your heart to healing.* Healing is definitely not something that happens easily or quickly. It is a process; but before you can begin the process, you must open your heart so that you can allow yourself to become healed. Many people choose to stay bitter rather than to receive healing. It is a choice; make the right one!

2. *Seek godly counsel.* Whether a professional Christian counselor, or a trusted Christian friend, talking to someone is part of the healing process. Remember you can always talk to the Wonderful Counselor, Jesus.

3. *Apply Scripture to your life situation.* God's Word is living and breathing and applies to every life situation that we will ever face. The more we can apply what God's Word says to our circumstance, the better equipped we will be for handling it. I personally have enjoyed memorizing Bible verses by writing them on index cards and keeping them tucked away in the pocket of my Bible. My Bible has a concordance in the back that matches a topic to a verse of Scripture. It is a wonderful tool, and learning Scripture has been at the core of my own healing process. Hence, all the Scripture references throughout this book.

4. *Forgive or release the person who hurt you.* Often in order to experience true healing, we need to have a forgiving heart. If the person who wronged you never

asks for forgiveness, release them to God. There is true freedom in forgiveness or release.

Key Scripture: **"'For if you forgive men when they sin against you, your heavenly Father will also forgive you. But if you do not forgive men their sins, your Father will not forgive your sins.'" Matthew 6:14-15**

5. *Allow time and Jesus to bind up your wounds.* With time and God's grace, you will eventually experience true healing. Let the only One who is able to completely heal your heart take His precious time. Surrender your heart to Him and trust Him to make good on His promises.

Key Scripture: **"He heals the brokenhearted and binds up their wounds." Psalm 147:3**

Endnotes

1. Stacy L. Bradford, "The Five Mistakes Married Women Make," SmartMoney, August 17, 2005, www.smartmoney.com.

2. Hal Lane, *Explore the Bible, Ruth, 1 Samuel, Adult Learner Guide Spring 2001,* (Nashville: Lifeway Christian Resources of the Southern Baptist Convention, 2000) 19.

3. Jaymes Song, "Kauai Dam Bursts," *Maui News,* 15 March 2006.

4. Dr. Gary Chapman, *The Five Love Languages of Apology,* (Chicago: Northfield Publishing, 2006) 142-143.

5. Beth Moore, *A Woman's Heart God's Dwelling Place,* (Nashville: Lifeway Press, 2007) 37.

Christy Long is available for speaking engagements and personal appearances. For more information contact:

Christy Long
C/O Advantage Books
P.O. Box 160847
Altamonte Springs, Florida   32716
christy@christylong.org

Comfort to Comfort Ministries
www.christylong.org.

To purchase additional copies of this book or other books published by Advantage Books call our toll free order number at:
1-888-383-3110 (Book Orders Only)

or visit our bookstore website at:
www.advbookstore.com

Longwood, Florida, USA
"we bring dreams to life"™
www.advbooks.com

www.ingramcontent.com/pod-product-compliance
Lightning Source LLC
LaVergne TN
LVHW091300080426
835510LV00007B/341